James C. All
2009

MW00464609

Went to Barbara Shepherds'
grandsons' school
for tribute to
ones who served
our country
in Combat

(Korea
1949-51

Served 13½ yrs.
active + Reserve

Oral F. "Tex" Lindsey

TOP TURRET

Mission Adventures of a B17 Flight Engineer

By

Oral F. Lindsey

authorHOUSE™

1663 LIBERTY DRIVE, SUITE 200
BLOOMINGTON, INDIANA 47403
(800) 839-8640
WWW.AUTHORHOUSE.COM

First published by AuthorHouse 03/22/05

ISBN: 1-4208-1237-8 (sc)
ISBN: 1-4208-1238-6 (dj)

Printed in the United States of America
Bloomington, Indiana

This book is printed on acid-free paper.

Also by Oral F. Lindsey: "A Soldier's Poems" 1993, 2003.

Cover Design by Jesi Wood.

Biblical Scripture marked (KJV) taken from the King James Version.

Scripture quotations marked (NLT) are from the New Living Translation © 1996 -Used by permission of Tyndale House Publishers, Inc., Wheaton, Illinois 60189. All Rights Reserved.

Compiled and edited by Virginia Norton.

TOP TURRET

BY ORAL F. LINDSEY

This book is dedicated to Elmer Farnsworth, Leon Cook, Walter Morrow, Chuck Himolka, and those soldiers like them who made the ultimate sacrifice for the sake of freedom – and to my daughter, Virginia Norton, without whom this book would have never been published.

Fact and Fiction

All literary work and information contained in this writing was compiled from the author's own experiences and accounts of events that he personally witnessed. The personal letters are reproductions of the original correspondence received.

Unless otherwise stated everything within this literary work is true and accurate to the best of the author's knowledge. In some instances names of individuals have been omitted and their rank alone was used.*

* *A Little Boy's Dream* is fiction and *A True Friend* is an expression of the author's personal conviction based on Biblical fact.

* *In the Beginning* – A soldier's name has been replaced with the fictitious name **Dirk**.

* *Replacement Crews* and *School of Hard Knocks* – **Collier** replaces the actual name of a new recruit.

* *Trial and Terror in Texas* – **Clackett** has been substituted for name of the commanding officer at Sheppard Field in Wichita Falls.

* *Mission Adventures II* – **Lieutenant Jackson** is a name used to protect the identity of the pilot mentioned in several stories.

INACCURACIES: Please contact us through the publisher if you should discover any inaccuracies or if you identify material that is not properly credited to its source.

IMAGES: Available photos, images, and articles were added where appropriate. These are intended to enhance not only the enjoyment, but also the historical value of this work. Photos that were not the personal property of the author have credit lines.

NOTE: Some information has been presented in more detail to offer a clearer understanding for those individuals that might not be familiar with the planes in this era or with military life

Acknowledgements

I gratefully acknowledge the following for their assistance and encouragement in the initiation and production of this book:

Associate Editor - Jennifer Norton spent countless hours providing her professional services while protecting the personal writing style of these candid stories.

Photo Research and Acquisition – William Norton had the most difficult assignment second only to editing. His extensive research of the internet resulted in corroborating facts to confirm the integrity of material covered in different stories. Many hours were also spent searching articles, books, photo collections, and the internet for those photos not directly available and then pursuing the artist or copyright holder to secure release for publication.

Additional Research - Wendy Marini conducted research on a wide range of information verifying names and dates and assuring accuracy as much as is humanly possible.

My son, Alan Lindsey, assisted in almost every area regarding the preparation and processing of the *Top Turret*. With his daily support and encouragement, and providing transportation, I was able to complete the book even through several admissions to the hospital.

Ruby Taylor, my daughter, initiated contact with the Commemorative Air Force which led to the additional writings and ultimately to the publication of this work.

I extend my sincere thanks to COL Robert W. Wood of the Commemorative Air Force, Arizona Wing, for taking an interest in the poems and making contact with Professor Watson at West Texas A&M on my behalf.

COL Don R. Watson, USA Ret., Professor and Director of Education for the Texas Aviation Historical Society, Director of the Aerospace Education Center and Museum at West Texas A&M University in Canyon, Texas. His belief in this project and assistance in connecting us with a publisher was a priceless contribution to getting the "Top Turret" in the book stores and to history enthusiasts everywhere.

Phyllis Grubbs is greatly appreciated for her creativity, professionalism, and personalized service. Phyllis Grubbs Photography - Abilene, Texas. All rights reserved.

I also want to thank those individuals from around the world who have posted messages on the World Wide Web offering their sincere expressions of gratitude to the men and women who served in WWII.

I want to also acknowledge those individuals and organizations that contribute time and resources unselfishly to keeping WWII history alive and available. I am amazed at the efforts across the country and in Europe of those that seek to acquire data, or record personal accounts, and especially those involved in the acquisition and restoration of WWII vintage airplanes (to keep them flying or as displays in museums). Thank you, again, for preserving history for us and generations to come.

Two excellent sources outside the official national and military arena are:

W. W. (Bill) Varnedoe Jr. and Frank Mays of the 385th Bomb Group and their support and development of the website: www.b17warhorse.com/html

Also, the 385th Bombardment Group Memorial Association and their production of the newsletter, *Hardlife Herald*, help the veterans from this group stay in touch while providing valuable information monthly. The contact for this publication is:

385th BGMA

Verne D. Philips, Treasurer

P.O. Drawer 5970

Austin, Texas 78763 USA

PHOTOS are captioned with Title and Credit Line or Acknowledgements

Whatever is good and perfect comes to us from God above,
who created all heaven's lights.
James 1:17a NLT

Foreword

This collection of short stories and poems is a picture window into WWII from the vantage point of a B-17 top turret gunner. The short stories relate actual accounts of this USAAF enlisted man's experiences from October of 1942 through June of 1945 as he prepared for and fought in the European Theatre of WWII. The tales describe everything from the most casual conversation spoken with comrades to dramatic and sometimes savage events that cannot be forgotten. Photos, images, and news articles enhance the facts by putting faces to names and credibility to the claims. Should this not be enough, the book concludes with letters from the past and present that place this book on a more personal level. One, specifically, is a poignant letter from an English lady to this soldier depicting her everyday life and making note of current events that turn this spontaneous communication into a virtual "time capsule".

Throughout his training and combat missions TSGT Oral F. Lindsey's steps were guarded by Divine providence, and each time tragedy struck, he was placed just out of harm's way. Images and events included in this historical treasure are simply a reflection of his heroism and character and reveal his faith in God.

It is our hope that this book will bring a realization to those post-war generations of the sacrifices made and the cruelty that is a part of every war. Letters from private citizens affected by WWII were included to reflect the gratitude of people around the world for America's servicemen and the US support of freedom everywhere.

Equally important was to honor these citizens by giving worldwide voice to their personal thoughts.

Scripture has been added that reflects the author's belief that God's holy word gives testimony to His presence in our lives. Some soldiers cast pennies into the North Sea for luck, but this airman cast his lot with the providence of God. And it is by His grace that this book was written, not to pose as a great literary work, but for future generations to have the chance to go back in time and see a view of WWII from the "Top Turret."

Virginia L. Norton

Oral Franklin Lindsey

Bless the Lord, who is my rock. He gives me strength for war and skill for battle. He is my loving ally and my fortress, my tower of safety, my deliverer. He stands before me as a shield, and I take refuge in him. He subdues the nations under me.
Psalm 144:1-2 NLT

Table of Contents

From Farming to Flying

In The Beginning

John Franklin Lindsey was my father's name. Before I was born my parents knew and respected a man named Oral. He was a policeman and had been a soldier of WWI. That is how my name came to be Oral Franklin Lindsey. I was born on April 30, 1922, the seventh of seven children. I probably was spoiled, but as the youngest child I experienced being last or left-out in a lot of situations. At least there was the advantage of learning from my three brothers and three sisters.

The names of all kinds of animals and birds on the farm were some of the first things I remember learning. The animals interested me much more than farming, but choices were out of the question. We all had to learn everything possible about the duties and responsibilities of farming and caring for livestock. I will skip the exciting years of chopping cotton and maize. During many months out of the year we would work twelve hours a day, six days a week unless one was on his deathbed. That's the way West Texas families and a lot of American families worked in that era of our society.

Now I must move on to my education. The school was about three and a half miles away, and we usually walked it both ways. It wasn't uphill both directions, but sometimes it seemed like it was. School wasn't that great, but I had a real passion for reading books. I read everything I could get my hands on – pirate stories and any sea adventures, the far north (particularly about Alaska), heroic war stories, books about Indians, Westerns, detective novels, and then finally, airplanes.

In my youth I played with rubber-shooting guns and any other weapon from the slingshot to swords. At school or at home our games were "cops and robbers," sword fighting, or wrestling. We also had knife throwing contests. Sometimes the playing ended in more serious competition. These situations gave me the opportunity to learn about self-preservation.

When I was a little older and had the chance, I would go hunting or just camping out. Guns had always been a part of life where I lived, but at first I had been troubled by the noise and the "kick" of firing a gun. Later, shooting became an enjoyable pastime for me. I never realized at the time that these experiences were more of a training field than a mere pastime.

During these years I learned how to build a campfire, track game, and find my way through the shinry (thicket). I worked on my aim with a rifle by hunting for small game. But on these excursions I was developing the discipline of patience and learning to use proper judgment such as what and when to shoot at a target. I also learned the importance of being prepared.

All of these were extremely valuable attributes that would help me later as a gunner in combat. I know these experiences helped me think more clearly in the face of gunfire even when fighting was heaviest and flak was bursting all around. Of course, my faith in God and His providence is what truly got me through the war. I believe that He expects us to develop what He has given us, then protects and provides in the moment of our weakness and for those things that are humanly impossible.

There is no way I can give enough credit to my mother and father for the early years of my life. The things they taught us are as true today as they were then. Mama and Papa were both real Christians, and the Bible was their law and love book. We were even told about wars, evil people, famine and other bad things in the world, though I didn't believe or understand much of it then. Their Christian influence, teachings, and the difficult farm life helped prepare me for demanding situations that would develop later in my life.

Teach your children to choose the right path,
and when they are older, they will remain upon it.
Proverbs 22:6 NLT

The Simple Days
Oral at age ten (far right) – seated on parents' 1931 Chevy

In my late teens I was really beginning to wonder about my future. Then, one day while reading the newspaper (in 1940 I believe) there was a newspaper article that really captured my attention. It described a new type of airplane that had been built called the B-10. I shared the story with my father and noted that they expected this giant ship to have a flight engineer, two pilots, and several gunners. It was late in 1941 before I got around to telling my father the interest I had in that plane. He was not much impressed that I wanted to be a flight engineer or a gunner on the already legendary bomber. He pointed out that it would probably require a college degree, and I only had a ninth-grade education. I never mentioned the airplane or my dreams again to my parents and gave up on the idea, at least for a time. But I continued to read everything I could find about the plane that had now become the B-17 Flying Fortress.

B-17 Flying Fortress

WWII Vintage Postcard – Courtesy of John Sullivan, Sr.

"For I know the plans I have for you," says the Lord.
"They are plans for good and not for disaster,
to give you a future and a hope.
Jeremiah 29:11 NLT

A Dream Revived

In the early part of the war, an outfit known as the "Old 19th" went down in recorded history as not doing too well with the B-17 bomber in battle. However, these brave men did the best they could in a very difficult situation. I would soon meet some of those men and would fight the Germans with some of them.

On the 19th of October, 1942, I went to Camp Walters at Mineral Wells, Texas, and enlisted in the Army. I explained that I was "good" with a rifle and wanted to be a sniper. Everyone took aptitude tests to reveal their potential skills. My counselor was a young captain who told me very seriously that snipers were killed quickly, regardless of their skill. He added that my mechanical aptitude was very high and that my best chance was to put in for mechanic school, then go on to gunnery school, after which I would be eligible for Boeing Flight Engineering School. It was like being struck by a bolt of lightning as the memory of a stifled dream was revived!

At Camp Walters I met Orville Knapp while we were standing in line to get our dog tags. He had also tested high in the area of mechanics and engineering. We would become very good friends as we went through training at various camps across the nation. Eventually, both of us ended up in England.

Take delight in the Lord,
and He will give you your heart's desires.
Psalm 37:4 NLT

Trial and Terror in Texas

Orville Knapp and I went first to basic training at Sheppard Field in Wichita Falls, Texas. There was the usual cursing and humiliation meted out to the new recruits. We would get as little as 36 hours sleep in a seven-day week. Once, I went 72 hours on about 10 hours of sleep. I would go to sleep in formation at the end of the day, but looking back it didn't seem that bad. I leaned on God and He carried me through the worst times. At least two of us, Knapp and I, did not mind so much, because we had our sights set on becoming flight engineers. We would talk about our goals but never mentioned this to the other recruits.

Sheppard Airfield had a reputation for being extremely successful at training aircraft mechanics. But there was more to that reputation. The base commander was supposedly a former general who had been busted to colonel and sent to Sheppard Field.

During a radio broadcast, I once heard Walter Winchell refer to the airfield as Colonel *Clackett's* Concentration Camp. Another recruit heard the broadcast when Winchell announced to parents not to worry about their sons going to war; instead, worry about them going to Sheppard Field in Texas.

At inspections Colonel Clackett always carried a croppy (or whip) and would crack it in the face of a recruit. If the kid cried, then he would go to the next man and inspect him. He stopped in front of me and when he found nothing wrong, he began to insult me and crack the whip in my face. I said to myself, "He can't break me." He kept getting closer to my eyes with each pop of the little

11

whip, but I managed to keep a poker face. As quickly as he had verbally attacked me, he was gone and never tried it with me again.

I saw him drive rookies more like he was torturing prisoners. On one particular training day we were climbing down a rope from a forty-foot wall. Standing at a distance I saw a young recruit fall from the top of the wall. I didn't observe him before the fall, but I assumed that he either got dizzy or fainted. Colonel Clackett stood over him cursing. The kid died right there on the ground just a few yards from me.

Captain McGinn was watching, and he grabbed the colonel by the arm and dragged him to his car and made him get in. He told the guards that Clackett was under house arrest. He shook his finger in Clackett's face and said, "You are under arrest, and I'm recommending you for a Court-Martial."

The very next day a one star general sneaked in dressed as a private and fell in line not far behind me. Captain McGinn had just given the men the orders of the day when this gentleman stepped out of formation. The captain told the "private" that if he would step back in line, he would be with him in a moment. The gentleman said, "I'm no private and you are hereby relieved of duty." The general was pinning his star on his uniform as he walked forward. Captain McGinn came to attention, saluted, and said, "Yes, sir." Then he was escorted away and put under arrest.

I will paraphrase the general's address to us: "This has nothing to do with McGinn's performance. I have all the confidence in the world in his abilities. However, I will be your commanding officer for the next few days and that's all I'm going to share with you. I believe I'm capable of filling the commanding position as well as a captain. I expect you sergeants to go about your duties, following the orders as Captain McGinn instructed. There should be nothing else discussed on these matters. Your job is to focus on your training and not concern yourself with this matter."

It wasn't long before Colonel Clackett was back in command at Sheppard. Some things I will never understand. Captain McGinn was not my ideal, but all the men I knew were pleased with his action against Clackett. Unfortunately, when a captain tries to overthrow a base commander, the odds are greatly against him.

But those who wait on the Lord will find new strength.
They will fly high on wings like eagles.
They will run and not grow weary.
They will walk and not faint.
Isaiah 40:31 NLT

Brainless Wonders

One hot afternoon just into our second week of basic training we were singled out of formation. "Knapp and Lindsey, fall out and report to the first sergeant," yelled the drill sergeant. Everyone started laughing. Being called off the drill field usually meant punishment of some sort was just ahead: KP, guard duty, or maybe even worse. It was definitely not a good sign, especially since Orville and I had been in trouble once before. It gave me no encouragement knowing that I hadn't been getting along with our barracks chief, a corporal who had just been busted.

This was something much more important and urgent. We were notified that we were being sent to Aircraft and Engine School. They had us scheduled to start on November 9, 1942. The sergeant explained that Knapp and I were being rushed through the process because engineers were so badly needed. Along with the news was a promise: "Your grades will have to be high or you'll end up just being a grease monkey."

The school was located on the same base, but Knapp and I were moved to another barracks. Soon we were in school and devoting ourselves to studying. Neither of us had attended college. I had only attended school through the ninth grade. This was not uncommon in our times, but we were competing with many college graduates. We must have appeared a little out of our league, as we were both small and underweight. Many service men would graduate from this school as aircraft or engine mechanics, so we never discussed with anyone else the plans that the military had for us.

Our scores were very high from the start, and upon completion Knapp and I were in the top ten percent of our class. We graduated from Sheppard Field Air Mechanic School on March 9th of 1943. About fifteen of us were then given orders to continue on to Seattle, Washington. Now that we had graduated with the credentials needed to attend Engineering school and we had our orders in hand, Knapp and I began to tell our friends about our goals. Most of the men we knew were shocked, some even horrified. "You'll be killed or captured your first week!"

One even said, "They won't take either of you two idiots on a B-17; they need somebody with brains."

I said to myself, "Well, thanks for the vote of confidence!"

On March 15th Orville Knapp and I left for our next training – twenty-eight days of schooling at Boeing's Flying Fortress School. We were promoted to the rank of corporal on March 25th and, brainless or not, there we were in Seattle eating the best chow in the military. They treated us like human beings and school was good. Compared to what we had just come through, it was like Heaven on Earth.

Again we were among the very few who had not attended college, and this course was really tough. Knapp and I just kept trudging along, hitting the books hard. It's amazing what determination and lots of studying can do because these "two idiots" graduated in the top ten percent . . . again! We graduated from Fortress school April 23rd and prepared to leave for Salt Lake City, Utah. Once more we heard a warning, "Wendover is the toughest of the gunnery schools."

This didn't shake our confidence now that our goal was almost in sight.

We were sent to Salt Lake City, that same day. We reached the Army-Air Base at Salt Lake on April 24th around 1:00 am. I volunteered to take the Gunner Examination and passed the test. Of course, Knapp took the test and passed too.

The next day I entered the low-pressure chamber and made it to 22,000 feet without oxygen and then on to 28,000 with oxygen. It caused my right ear to bother me some, but everything else was fine. Knapp had gone through the chamber test the day before me. Now that we had completed these requirements, it was time for another school. On May 11th we left for Wendover Aerial Gunnery School.

The wise person makes learning a joy; fools spout only foolishness.
Proverbs 15:2 NLT

United States Army

Air Forces Technical Command

AIRPLANE MECHANICS SCHOOL

Be it known that

Corporal Oral F. Lindsey

has satisfactorily completed the course
as prescribed by the Army Air Forces and given at the

ARMY AIR FORCES TRAINING DETACHMENT

BOEING FLYING FORTRESS SCHOOL

In testimony whereof and by virtue of vested authority
I do confer upon him this

——DIPLOMA——

Given on this   23rd   *day of*   April

in the year of our Lord one thousand nine hundred and   forty-three.

HOLTON H. PRIBBLE, Captain, Air Corps.
COMMANDING OFFICER

Official Photograph US Army Air Corps

Base Photographic Section

Army Air Base, Wendover, Utah

Forged in the Desert Heat

Wendover Field, Utah – Aerial Gunnery School began on May 17, 1943. For the first few days it was somewhat like basic training, but very soon we were into the serious business. The training was hard. For conditioning purposes they put us on water rationing for the first two weeks. Water was available at meal times, but we were only allowed to fill our one-quart canteens three times each day. In 120 degree desert heat the body can go through a lot of fluids, and some of us just didn't feel that we could get by on this small amount of water.

We moved into a tent after spending three days out under the desert sky, and there I met Eric and Johnny. Eric was small built like Knapp and me, but Johnny was as big and tough as the rest of us were small and skinny. Our first night was a bad one in the tent. We were starved for water. Knapp and I decided to steal water even with a guard on the water tank day and night. Eric said it was against his religion, and Johnny said that he was too slow to get by with it.

For about a week Knapp or I went out and succeeded in stealing water each night. We tried a different scheme each time. Once I walked through the N.C.O. barracks, put on a sergeant's coat, filled up six canteens and retraced my steps through the same barracks since no one was there. Knapp got caught going through that same barracks and was asked, "What are you doing here?"

Glancing down at a name tag on a bunk he responded, "Looking for Sgt. Baker, Sir." Of course Baker was not there. Knapp was able to complete his mission and returned with the canteens full of water.

There were other escapades while we were off duty. Like the time another buddy of mine, Liner, went with me on a hike up the mountains. We wanted to get a look at Salt Lake City. It was about a hundred miles away, but from the mountaintops we were told it looked more like it was only twenty. We set our sights for the tallest peak and began the trek up the mountain.

There was a huge boulder that capped this mountain and once we reached the top we were able to climb up on it giving us a great view of Salt Lake City. After looking around a bit Liner and I took a break and sat down. That's when we noticed a smaller rock on top of the boulder. It appeared to have been placed there because it sat so flush and level. If it had been put there by someone, then who and why?

We took a closer look and decided to move the rock because of its unusual position. When we rolled the stone over we found the most amazing thing! This rock had a unique cavity in it and was perfectly covering a slight depression in the larger stone. And in this secret hiding place was a Bible! There wasn't a name or any markings in the Bible that would indicate where it came from or who might have placed it there. It wasn't damaged or weathered.

It showed absolutely no sign of exposure to water or dampness. In the mountains one could expect there to be high winds along with rains and snow in season. It's reasonable to believe that the Bible would have gotten wet unless this stone was a perfect fit! Liner and I took some time to flip through the Bible and read some passages before replacing it exactly as we had found it. Looking back on this memory it seems to have a familiar ring: we had *rolled away the stone* and found the *Word of God.*

As if this unique adventure wasn't enough to write home about, we would have a different type of excitement just ahead. Liner and I began our descent down the side of the mountain in a gully that had been created from the runoff of heavy rains. This gully became more of a ravine that grew deeper and more defined as we reached the foot of the mountain. Making our way down we noticed some men from camp walking through the trees that covered the lower part of the ravine. They were headed along the only pathway back to camp.

It only took a matter of minutes to reach the bottom of the ravine but the men we had just seen were not in sight. Then we heard a crackling sound and saw that the cedars just ahead of us were on fire. The winds that swirled around the tree tops were spreading the fire quickly while the cedars provided their own fuel. It didn't take long for us to realize we had no chance of escaping through the trees and there didn't appear to be any other options.

We couldn't return up the mountain by way of the washout. It was so steep and rugged that we wouldn't be able to stay ahead of the growing inferno. We didn't have much time to find a way out. Liner and I worked together quickly to find the most promising point on the ravine wall to make our escape. I was smaller than Liner, so he was able to hoist me high enough that I could get hold of some brush and pull myself up and over the top ridge.

By now the fire was dangerously close. I found a really long branch and lowered it to Liner. He didn't think I could hold him, but I screamed for him to grab hold and start climbing. As he took hold of the branch and began to climb, the radiating heat from the fire was intensifying. As soon as Liner was out of the ravine, he quickly stripped off his shirt. It was so hot that he thought it was on fire. Fortunately it was only scorched, but a few seconds more and it would have burst into flames. Liner said if we hurried he thought we could catch those scoundrels. He was ready to kill somebody, and I couldn't blame him.

We finally reached camp and I examined Liner's back. We were both amazed to find that his back was not burned even though his shirt was ruined. He didn't have to report to the infirmary and we never made an official report of the incident. One thing was clear to us. We believed it was miracle – we were delivered safely from the fire by the same divine providence that placed the Bible under the stone.

Liner and I did ask around about men that might have been seen running into camp. No one saw anyone as we described, nor admitted to knowing of any suspicious behavior. I told him that it would do no good even if we could catch them. We couldn't prove that the fire was set deliberately, and this gang undoubtedly would stick together to deny everything.

Liner and I hoped that our bodies would recover by morning. I felt strange that night sitting on my bunk and trying to mentally prepare for the next day. This wasn't the only time that my biggest concern had nothing to do with tests or training. It seems the most difficult challenges in life always deal with personal or professional relationships.

The bully of our outfit was a big Norwegian kid that I will call Dirk. He had beaten two of the men so badly that they were in critical condition and almost died. He fought with his feet and would stomp a man once he had him down.

I was harassed by Dirk continuously throughout gunnery school. Nothing could be done about it, so I avoided him like the plague. Finally, my sergeant told me, "You'll have to fight him if you want to put an end to this."

I was thinking to myself, "Oh, great advice. That would *end it* alright!" Dirk outweighed me by at least forty pounds, and undoubtedly he would take me down in short order. And I didn't want to get set back in my schooling just because this moose thought I needed my face rearranged. I calculated that at the very least I would sustain a severe beating, and I could be laid up for a week or maybe two. So I decided to endure his insults and abuse until we completed all of the requirements for graduation from gunnery school.

After graduation word was spreading around camp that Dirk was looking for me, so when I encountered him it was no accident. He cursed me and insulted me as usual, but this time I answered with a challenge. While I moved into position as if to fight him bare knuckled, he charged me like a madman. I had no plans to fist fight this buffalo, but then I also hadn't planned on his being quite so eager.

The other men must have been thinking, "Lindsey really is an idiot!" But I just remained focused, and when Dirk was within my reach, I took hold of him. Then I stepped back, crouched down a bit, and shoved my knee right into his midriff. I fell backward, and using his momentum and weight, I threw him over me. He sailed gracefully over me but landed on the railing of an army bunk with no mattress to pad his fall. His back was injured so badly that it never healed during the next year that we were stationed together.

Looking back I always regretted the incident. This certainly hadn't been my plan, but Dirk could no longer bully others like he had always done before. I decided that maybe my sergeant had more insight than I had given him credit for.

Although the conditions at Wendover were grueling, we were fortunate to have really good instructors. Before we left we had learned to field strip and re-assemble a .50 caliber machine gun blindfolded. We learned to shoot them, too, but our practice wasn't enough to prepare us for war. Graduation from here would mean buck sergeant stripes, a pair of silver wings, and orders to flight training on B-17's.

I graduated on June 25th and was presented with my silver wings and diploma by a nurse who was a first lieutenant. Right after receiving sergeant stripes and silver wings, a group of us were assigned to three nights of KP duty. Achievement and confidence are always short-lived in the military.

We left Wendover on the second of July, and as the train pulled out we looked beyond the little camp up in the hills. Tracers could be seen from the time they left the guns 'til they burned out against a mountainous backdrop. Another chapter in my life was closing, and in one brief moment I made up a short verse and sang it aloud –

Good-Bye Wendover Utah,
You've been kind to me.
You gave me a pair of silver wings
And a stripe to make me three.

It's strange business, this life in the service. Part of it you like and part of it is unbearable. I was glad I got in, but I would be just as glad when it came time to get out. Our train left Salt Lake on the ninth of July. Our first stop was Spokane, Washington. After a layover there we reached our final destination, Moses Lake, on the twelfth of July.

When you go through deep waters and great trouble,
I will be with you.
When you go through rivers of difficulty, you will not drown!
When you walk through the fire of oppression,
you will not be burned up;
The flames will not consume you.
Isaiah 43:2 NLT

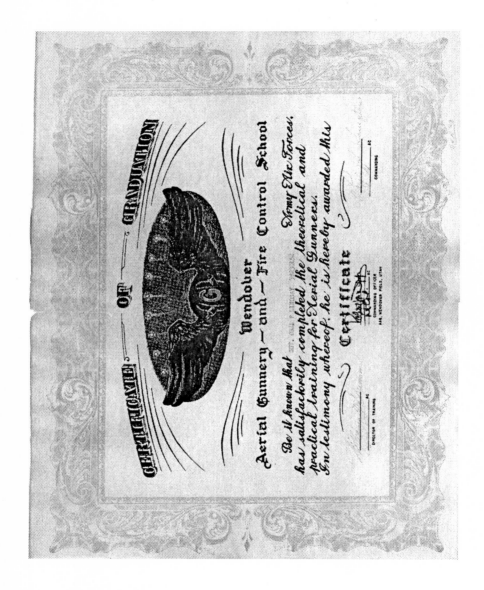

A Crew Is Formed Despite Tragedy

Those that graduated gunnery school were sent to Moses Lake, Washington, where we went through flight training and the crews were formed. Knapp and I had been training to be flight engineers so Moses Lake is where we parted ways – each assigned to a different crew and in separate squadrons.

At first my crew (Crew 29) consisted only of Edward Leach and me. Soon Leroy Bevins, Albert Baumann, and Johnny Colston were added. The last enlisted man added to the group was Arthur Yielding. On our next formation a young lieutenant named William Clark was introduced to us as the crew's first pilot, and another gentleman, Lieutenant Jennings, as our co-pilot. Richard Wheaton was designated as our bombardier and Dexter Schleusener as navigator. This completed our original crew. I emphasize *original* because soon changes would be made.

I was offered the position of flight engineer, flying top turret. I was reluctant because Leach had experience and more education, but with his encouragement I accepted. This was my dream and I was thankful that he wanted me to take the position. Leach took the positions of assistant engineer and ball turret gunner; Bevins, left waist gunner and armorer; Baumann, right waist gunner; and Colston would be our tail gunner. Yielding was radio-operator and had the top ring-mounted .50 caliber.

We flew several training missions. All members were advancing very well when Baumann, Bevins, and I were sent to Camp Seven Mile for advanced gunnery training. We were being scored on our abilities, and this would literally make or break our status on the crew. We immediately beat all competition at everything from the Browning .50 caliber machine guns to the Colt .45 pistol. Baumann was an accomplished skeet shooter. Bevins, a Virginian country boy, was good with almost any type of weapon and was also a real specialist on the turrets. I was best with a rifle but could also shoot a shotgun and pistol fairly well. I had already beaten all the others in training at Wendover with the good ole top turret guns.

The last event of the day was the top turret simulation. A shotgun was positioned on the gun mount of a top turret and a clay pigeon was catapulted at high speed to somewhat simulate shooting at a fighter. We were given one shotgun shell to break the clay. The grueling challenge went for 25 rounds. Each soldier was given 25 pigeons and 25 shot-shells. Bevins and I broke every clay pigeon thrown for us, resulting in a tie for top score.

After our successful competition, we learned of a tragic failure. Lieutenant Clark and the rest of our crew had crashed during a training flight the night before in the mountains not far from Spokane. They had defective gasoline gauges and ran out of gas, forcing everyone to bail out. Clark had a long gash down his back from a tree limb that caught him as he was landing. Schleusener's chute was caught in a tree and he was left hanging over a canyon. He cut his harness and was able to swing over to safety virtually unscathed. Wheaton was bruised up a bit but nothing serious. Leach lost his shoes and landed barefoot in the rocks, but he wasn't critical either. They were fortunate, but that wasn't true for everyone that night.

Lieutenant Jennings' landing tumbled him down onto a steep rocky mountainside. Bailing out in darkness made it impossible to see a potentially safe place to land. Doctors at first thought he might not ever walk again. He took a severe beating, which left him with about sixty different fractures in bones over his body. As a result, we lost a really good co-pilot.

Yielding's situation was even worse. He had been at the radio table when the order to bail out was given. The plane went down making a decent landing considering how rough the terrain was in this area. But it came in at a steep glide and rendered a powerful jolt when it hit. Clark found Yielding in the wreckage still strapped in his chair. He had ridden the fort down, and upon impact his chest was crushed. He died soon after Clark reached him. It was a training experience that cost us dearly.

Our training continued with the immediate assignment of co-pilot Second Lieutenant Paul Starr and a new radio operator, Staff Sergeant Lawrence Stanley (later replaced by Sanders). After completion we went on to Camp Kilmer, New Jersey, and soon boarded the Queen Elizabeth, which would take us to Glasgow, Scotland.

God's ways are as hard to discern as the pathways of the wind,
and as mysterious as a tiny baby being formed
in a mother's womb.
Ecclesiastes 11:5 NLT

Photograph Courtesy USAAF – Crew 6 (Declassified)

Standing Left to Right:
Johnny Colston, Edward Leach, Leroy Bevins, Oral Lindsey,
Albert Baumann, Laurence Stanley

Bottom Row Left to Right:
Richard Wheaton, Dexter Schleusener,
Paul Starr, William Clark

Voyage on the Queen Elizabeth

There was silence among the men as we waited to board the famous Queen Elizabeth. Everyone was tired but also overwhelmed by the moment. Armed guards were strategically stationed around us and other guards could be seen at the ship's railing. It was dark and all that I could really see was the general shape of this gigantic liner with her smoke stacks pointing to the night sky.

We stood four abreast, but each soldier stepped onto the gang plank alone and walked single file up to the gateway to the ship's deck. At this checkpoint an armed guard would halt the soldier while another guard marked a number on the man's forehead. When I reached the top to receive my number the guard shone his light and made his mark. Either the guard was becoming more zealous or I was just thin-skinned. As I heard him say 'move on' I felt the blood running down my face. I lifted my bags and followed the men ahead of me as blood dripped from my face onto my uniform.

My good friend Al Baumann was right in line with me. Soldiers were being directed off into different directions so we took the opportunity to step back away from the crowd. We were able to slip behind some structure or equipment on the deck where we could hide. Once everyone was on board the ship was towed away from the docks and soon the Queen Elizabeth was underway.

Our eyes were locked on the Statue of Liberty as she slowly sank into the ocean. It was like rolling over a large mountain of water while everything behind us disappeared from view. I was looking forward to this new adventure and it proved true – there was never a dull moment.

The second day at sea, an old man wearing civilian clothes climbed to the top rail; looking out to sea, he said something inaudible to us and then jumped overboard. When the ship's captain was told, he just nodded his head in recognition of the report. With over 24,000 troops on their way to war, he knew he could not turn around. If a boat had been dropped to the man, he could not have saved himself while weighed down with his clothing – he even wore an overcoat. When we realized that he was going to jump, I was less than ten yards from him but could not move fast enough to stop him.

We never even knew his name or why he was desperate enough to take his own life. Even if all conditions had been favorable for a rescue, and if we had been on a vessel that could maneuver quickly, it is doubtful that this poor soul could have been found in the rough waters. He most likely would have died from injuries sustained in the fall if he survived the impact of hitting the water. And with the heavy clothing and shoes he would have sunk quickly.

In spite of this tragedy, I have many pleasant memories of that fantastic voyage, including the view of the stars at night and the beautiful sunsets. But the thing I remember most was exploring the ship itself. One day I was drawn by the low rumbling of the huge diesel engines that powered the great ship. Following the sound, I made my way to the entrance of the engine room. It was a restricted area, so I was concerned about being caught. But I couldn't resist a look, so I just opened the door and peeked in. Immediately, a sailor noticed me and said, "Well, come on in." Once inside, the sailor introduced me to the whole crew. I explained that I had been assigned to a B-17 crew as the flight engineer, so they proceeded to tell me all about the three great diesel engines.

For years I had dreamed about being a flight engineer and experiencing the adventures that I was sure would be in store for me, but I never realized there would be many other exciting escapades and new discoveries to explore.

The heavens tell of the Glory of God.
The skies display his marvelous craftsmanship.
They speak without a sound or a word;
their voice is silent in the skies;
yet their message has gone out
to all the earth, and their words to all the world.
Psalm 19:1,3,4 NLT

RMS Queen Elizabeth
Photo Courtesy of www.LuxuryLinerRow.com

Destination Great Ashfield

After arriving in Glasgow, Scotland, we were shuttled over to the gunnery range in Snettisham for some final training. Snettisham is a terrible place in winter for rain, wind, and mud. However, the training facility was well set up and even had an indoor pistol range, although that was off limits for us.

I held the top score with the .30 caliber in this competition with gunners from many other squadrons. An Englishman overheard our crew discussing the results and claimed that I was just a braggart. So I asked the range master to let me shoot my .45 colt at the indoor range. The locals here were very proud of this indoor range, which was designed to provide the best in training, namely for the men of Scotland Yard. I believed these proud RAF Officers were expecting and even hoping that it would not be allowed. Nevertheless, when he agreed to open up the range for this demonstration, a group of eager spectators followed us through the mud.

Everyone quietly waited as the range master set up five man-sized targets which were standard for this drill in the training of officers for Scotland Yard. I was impressed by the prestige of the facility but not intimidated. I focused on preparing for the first exercise. The targets were set at a distance of fifteen feet. They pivoted, facing me for only two seconds. In those two seconds I shot all five silhouettes with scoring hits. The men watching thought this must be a fluke and insisted that I try again. Reluctantly, I submitted to their badgering. On this round I made four clean hits, but the last target was just swinging back as I hit it. There was a two-inch gash across the target where the bullet had skid through the paper as it turned. Someone there said that only fifty percent of the Scotland Yard officers ever scored on all five targets even after training at the facility. After that there was no more name-calling.

From there we went to the 385th Bomb Group stationed in Great Ashfield, England. We arrived at night and learned that the base had been hit that day with thermite bombs. Thermite is a mixture of iron oxide, powdered aluminum, and magnesium which burns with an intense heat that can melt even most metals. The runway sustained significant damage. Our first mission would be delayed until the repairs were done.

You must make allowance for each other's faults
and forgive the person who offends you.
Remember, the Lord forgave you,
so you must forgive others.
Colossians 3:13 NLT

Photograph Courtesy USAAF – (Declassified)

Standing Left to Right:
Albert Baumann, Dexter Schleusener, William Clark,
Paul Starr, Leroy Bevins

Bottom Row Left to Right:
Harry Sanders, Oral Lindsey, Johnny Colston, Edward Leach

Mission Adventures
First Tour

Initiation Day

It was a fine winter's day in England, cool but not cold. The date was December 16, 1943. Though it was in the middle of a mighty war, there was little here to prove it. The Blitz was over and the Royal Air Force was paying back the old debt at night while the U.S. Air Force operations led the daylight missions.

Great Fires Left In Blitzed Bremen

A fleet of Flying Fortresses and Liberators pounded Bremen in daylight early yesterday and left huge fires spreading across the already heavily blitzed city which is Germany's most important seaport.

Twenty-five bombers, five American fighters and three Spitfires, which carried out diversionary sweeps, were reported missing from the day's operations. Bomber gunners claimed 21 enemy aircraft destroyed.

Smoke Visible 50 Miles

As the bomber formations began the homeward leg of the 800-mile round trip, they could see huge fires spreading in the port area of the city and columns of smoke were visible 50 miles away above the haze of ground smoke put out by the defenses. Visibility was almost unlimited.

The bombers flew through a concentrated barrage of flak to carry out their fourth announced attack on Bremen since Nov. 13. In addition, German radio said five days ago that Bremen had been hit by U.S. bombers, but the USAAF announced only that targets in northwestern Germany were attacked that day.

Bremen, which has been pounded five times within 37 days by the USAAF, became the Reich's most important port after Hamburg was blasted out of existence by the combined attacks of RAF and U.S. heavy bombers last summer.

The big dock and shipbuilding areas are its most important targets, but the Focke Wulf repair factory, large textile works, grain mills and lumber yards also are prime military objectives.

The largest shipyards are those of the Deutsche Schiffwerke and the Deschimag Werke. Bremen's population has been swollen by its war-time importance to something more than 350,000, but how many of these have been driven from the city by the heavy pounding is not known. Swedish news reports repeatedly have told of civilian workers fleeing the ravaged city.

Of the seven attacks on Bremen which (Continued on page 4)

Raids - - - -

(Continued from page 1)

Eighth Bomber Command has announced since last April, two officially were described as aimed at the big Focke Wulf works, and the others at port and industrial facilities.

Bombers went to Bremen once in April, once in June, once in October, three times in November—13th, 16th, 29th—and once in December.

"It looks as though we did a tremendous amount of damage," said Col. Maurice A. Preston, of Dulare, Cal., a B17 combat wing commander, who led one of yesterday's Fortress formations.

"It is certainly one of the best operations we have ever had. I saw our bombs dropping right in the target area."

"I followed our bombs all the way down until they struck," said Sgt. Walter R. Cyr, of Tacoma, Wash., a ball turret gunner on the Fort Miami Clipper. "There were a lot of fires burning in Bremen, sending up big clouds of smoke."

Heavy Flak Encountered

M/Sgt. A. W. Gibbons, of Jamaica Plains, Mass., a navigator formerly with the RAF, said, "It was the heaviest concentration of flak I have ever seen."

It was the sixth day this month of operations for Eighth Bomber Command. Other attacks were on Dec. 1, 5, 11, 13 and 16, but only two targets of the first five were announced—Solingen and Emden; two of the others were described as "on northwestern Germany" and one on military installations in France.

THE STARS AND STRIPES
Daily Newspaper for U.S. Armed Forces – European Theater of Operations New York, N.Y. – London, England

To our crew, today was very significant. We were preparing for our first combat mission! Yes, our first, and it would certainly be no milk run, for the mission was to Bremen, Germany, one of the worst flak targets on the map. We would not be immune to fighter attacks either. Bremen was a name that sent chills down the spine of the experienced combat soldier. But to me it meant one thing – a testing ground for courage. The one thing a soldier fears the most is his own fear.

We had another change to our crew. Staff Sergeant Lawrence Stanley, our radio operator, was replaced at the last minute with Tech Sergeant Harry Sanders. This was to be our permanent crew throughout my first tour in Europe.

I was engineer and top turret gunner on the crew and held the rank of staff sergeant, but this reflected only my efficiency and willingness to work. I knew I might not be worth a dime in a high altitude air battle where a cool head is imperative to a man's very existence. It would be 55 degrees below zero over Bremen that day, and the anti-aircraft flak would be a solid box for forty miles. The Germans were firing 150mm shells that would be breaking up all around, throwing small pieces of steel in all directions. These pieces of debris could literally rip an arm or leg off a man's body.

Fighters with six or eight machine guns firing straight ahead would be in the game, too. They would fly straight at the same plane and let go with those murderous guns, and that plane's gunners would shoot back with everything they had. Odds were that at least one of the planes would be significantly damaged and some mother's son would likely fall across his guns, never to see home again.

I was observing all this but trying to shield myself from the reality. I was preparing for the mission with an optimistic attitude in spite of the trauma. After much help from the ground crew and what seemed to be a load of unnecessary work on our own part, we were in the air on time.

We were soon over the North Sea flying in formation headed for Bremen. Ten miles out to sea the other ships' crews began test-firing their guns, and immediately the newcomers followed up. I turned the top turret to the right rear and fired a short burst of "fifties" into thin air. The guns operated as smooth as silk, and the other gunners on board were almost as successful. After a few minutes all guns were working well. The enemy coast was soon in full view with enemy cannons ready and waiting.

The planes, still climbing, turned to hit the coastline straight on and avoid as much flak as possible. The twenty-one ship formation was now attached to two other similar formations to make up the Fourth Combat Wing of the Third Division of the Eighth Air Force. We were to attack a target, in broad daylight, that was well-fortified even against night attacks. Flak was light at the coast, and the hours dragged by monotonously as the formations bore deeper into the enemy's homeland. The formations were now heading toward the flak with bomb bay doors open and coming downwind at an altitude of 29,500 feet.

I felt a real shiver that was associated with both fear and the deadly cold. I had no parachute on, so I decided to remove the seat strap from the turret. This seemed to me somewhat safer – knowing that I would be able to escape swiftly from my post to reach my parachute in the event of a bailout.

NOTE: *The top turret, like the ball turret, was too small for a gunner to wear a parachute. Instead, I wore a harness onto which a chest pack chute could be quickly snapped. I would secure my chest pack on the floor of the plane. In the event of a bailout the chute could then be easily retrieved and snapped on.*

My nerves were calmer now, and I was thinking more clearly – clearly enough to see the insanity of flying straight and level into a mass of cannon fire like this! Then, reality seemed to be suspended as I saw a fort hit squarely in its mid-section. The B-17 broke up and fell like a glass bottle shattered by a bullet. Reality resumed suddenly at the sound of a shell bursting under the open bomb bay. Fragments hit the big demolition bombs and tore holes in the thin skin of the airplane as if they were ripping through a tin can. Another shell burst high in front of us and pelted our ship with a shower of small fragments. We heard many more small blasts, and several more B-17s went down within our sight.

Dick Wheaton, the bombardier, concentrated on his task and patiently waited for the target to come into view. When the plane was in position, he calmly pulled the switch, sending five one-thousand pound bombs on the docks of Bremen. At the age of twenty-one this successful mission was only his first. In time he would lead a total of twenty-one missions and never missed his mark.

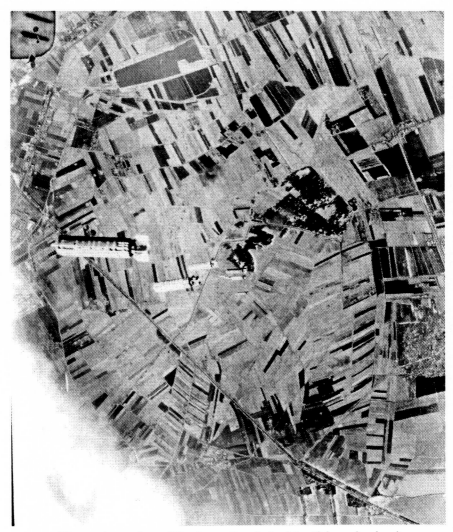

(Sample only – Photo not related to this mission)
USAAF Photo from Mr. Lindsey's Personal Collection

We had a 100-mile tail wind and were flying 180 mph air speed. At 30,000 feet you add another 60 mph because of the thin air, so our ground speed was about 340 miles per hour. As the ship rose from the release of 5,000 pounds of weight, somebody called out over the intercom, "Let's get the hell out of here!"

I don't remember just how many B-17's I personally saw go down, but many more would be lost because of battle damage. Most of those that didn't make it back had lost fuel from flak holes in the gas tanks, and some no doubt suffered mechanical maladies such as engine failure. The mission started with 400 B-17's, and forty of them were lost in this horrendous battle. Later, officers would tell us we were fortunate to have experienced a bad mission first. To be certain, we had been properly initiated and now felt prepared for just about anything.

Walter Cronkite was the most famous of The Writing 69th wartime journalists. He had this to say after flying on one of the missions:

"American Flying Fortresses have just come back from an assignment to hell; a hell 26,000 feet above the earth, a hell of burning tracer bullets and bursting gunfire, of crippled Fortresses and burning German fighter planes, of parachuting men and others not so lucky. I have just returned with a Flying Fortress crew from Wilhelmshaven.

(He continued)

Actually the first impression of a daylight bombing mission is a hodge-podge of disconnected scenes – things like bombs falling past you from the formation above, a crippled bomber with smoke pouring from one engine thousands of feet below – a Focke Wulf peeling off somewhere above and plummeting down shooting its way through the formation."

(Quote - The Writing 69th website – Spons. by Green Harbor Publications.)

I will bring that group through the fire and make them pure,
just as gold and silver are refined and purified by fire.
They will call on my name, and I will answer them.
Zechariah 13:9 NLT

Oral F. Lindsey

Friday, Feb. 11, 1944

Giant Air Duel

Hordes of Fighters Fail to Stop Blow at Nazi Aircraft Plants

Terrific Dogfights Develop; New Luftwaffe Tactics Force Some U.S. Escorts Back

THE STARS AND STRIPES
Daily Newspaper for U.S. Armed Forces – European Theater of Operations New York, N.Y. – London, England

Flying Fortresses, striking a new blow in the concerted pre-invasion campaign to wipe the Luftwaffe from the skies, yesterday smashed through some of the heaviest fighter opposition yet encountered to carry out the Eighth Air Force's third heavy blow in 30 days on Brunswick, where a large portion of Germany's warplanes are produced.

The Luftwaffe, judging from early reports of returning American crews, hurled everything it had into a desperate—but vain—effort to keep the bombers away from the target.

For 2½ hours—from the time the Forts roared across the enemy coast for the 450-mile penetration to Brunswick, until they reached the Channel again on the way back—the bombers and their escorts blazed away continuously at swarms of German fighters. Many said it was the roughest mission yet for the U.S. heavies, and others ventured the observation that the Luftwaffe must have had orders to halt the attack at any cost.

Direct Hits on Targets

No official announcement of bombing results or its losses had been made at Eighth Air Force headquarters late last night, but preliminary reports of crew members indicated that the great central Germany aircraft manufacturing center had received a severe pounding. Direct hits upon the targets were reported.

Fortress bombing "raised hell in the center of the target" despite the heavy opposition, crew members said.

Desperately striving to avert another crippling blow at its waning strength, the Luftwaffe appeared to have marshaled every fighter and used every tactic to stop the Fortresses. Ferocious dogfights raged between Allied and enemy fighter planes as the bombers plodded steadfastly toward Brunswick.

Many as 200 at One Time

Attacking the Forts themselves were never less than 75 fighters and sometimes as many as 200, said crews at one base. Sometimes German fighters 15 abreast plunged in at the bombers, while others dived through the formations in line from astern.

Hundreds of Me109s, FW190s and Ju88s mixed it up with the escorting Thunderbolts, Lightnings and Mustangs.

One new trick reported in use by the

(Continued on page 4)

51

Character Builder

The first mission to Bremen was, as I said, the heaviest flak we ever encountered. On December 20, 1943, we returned to Bremen. This time flak was again heavy but still less than before. Having fewer German fighters this time and more B-17's made this a much easier mission. But the cold was always there; 60 below to 75 below zero was order of the day. Your physical capabilities drop along with the extreme temperatures. Battling this cold takes away your courage, and it would take away your spirit if it were possible.

On January 7, 1944, we went to Ludwigshaven, making another seven hour mission. The cold still haunted us, but we were thankful for much less flak and fighters. On January 14th we went to Belmesnel, a real "milk run" of three and a half hours. Our assignment on January 21st was a cross bow target in France. Mission running time was five and one half hours with no opposition. On the 24th of January we flew to France on a special assignment which is detailed later in this book in the story *Bordeaux*.

On February 3rd we were sent to Wilhelmshaven, Germany, for a routine mission. Then on February 6th the target was St. Andre de L'Eure – an airfield less than fifty miles to the west of Paris, France. As with the last mission, we experienced only nominal flak and saw few fighters.

February 8th would bring lots of action, but it ended in success. At Frankfurt, Germany, we met hard fighter opposition, and the Germans fought us right through their own flak. But the guns of the Flying Fortresses were too much for the now weakened Luftwaffe.

The success of this mission was short-lived, however, for there would be plenty of grief ahead.

FORMATION FLYING THROUGH FLAK
USAAF Photo – Oral Lindsey's Personal Collection

On the tenth of February we received our orders and formation position for our mission to Brunswick. At this point in the war, daylight bombing had become much more successful due to formation strategy, which I will attempt to describe here. A division is made up of three wings, and each wing consists of three bomb groups. The three bomb groups in our wing were the 385th, the 447th, and the 94th group. The bomb groups were staggered by direction and by altitude. The 447th Bomb Group flew in the lead position with the 94th flying low and off to one side of them. Our bomb group, the 385th, was designated high position, and would be flying on the opposite side of the 447th from the 94th.

Within each group, one squadron of B-17's would be flying the far outside point, known as "Tail-End Charlie." Some considered, therefore, that three of these squadrons existed – one for each group within a wing. But there was only one "Tail-End Charlie" designated for the entire wing formation.

On this mission, my squadron, the 550th, would be flying the high, far-right position. Thus, we were "Tail-End Charlie" of the wing formation on this mission. This position was the most exposed to attack, making it one of the most dangerous. Groups and squadrons were rotated to take turns in this hot spot.

A write-up in the paper said that 200 enemy fighters were up that day. The enemy came at us in chow-line formation. We were hit by a pack of fighters from the right side of the formation. Three out of the first four Messerschmitt 109's were shot down.

Apparently they got the message, because the rest of the fighters peeled off and moved to the 94th Bomb Group. I believe that the 94th lost thirteen of their twenty-one ship formation that day.

Other fighters tried our squadron again and again; leaving bullet holes in every B-17 in the 550th, but not one plane was lost. In the heavy fighting, some of our men were wounded, and I believe one in our squadron was killed. I do know that God gave us that victory, for it was a miracle that we didn't have many more casualties. For most of us, this was our first real hard fight.

After this mission I looked at that bunch of men differently. I can't explain the change except that it was a character builder for sure. Our crew alone fired 8,000 rounds of .50 caliber ammo. Would you believe that not one of our men claimed a fighter? There had been many gunners throughout the squadron cranking out a veritable wall of bullets. How could one claim that it was his bullet that shot the enemy plane down?

Later we would take part in a critical battle that would break the back of Goering's Luftwaffe. The mission involved multiple targets and 2000 American planes against everything the Germans had to offer. We were assigned a safer spot in the formation and missed engaging in some of the more grueling attacks experienced by other squadrons. But as the story "Bail Out or Fall Out" will reveal, we did take enough hits to have our own crisis.

We can rejoice, too, when we run into problems and trials, for we know that they are good for us – they help us learn to endure. And endurance develops strength of character in us, and character strengthens our confident expectation of salvation.
Romans 5: 3-4 NLT

On Overload

We had not been at Great Ashfield very long when we got the opportunity to have a day off. On this particular day, Roy, Al, and I decided to watch the planes taking off. We were standing on a vacant hard-stand when we noticed a B-17 developing a problem. We heard its engines roar and all the superchargers scream as it started takeoff. The plane looked alright, and when the wheels left the ground we thought they had it made. However, it settled back down just after the end of the runway and skidded a short distance. Then the plane suddenly stopped cold and burst into flames. None of the crew escaped.

The B-17 had a full gas load and was carrying ten 500 lb. bombs. All ten bombs exploded together. I saw what looked like a giant halo, which reached us in about a second. I had just witnessed my first explosion shockwave. This is the force that bends and twists steel beams, knocks down stone walls, and scrambles men's insides.

Roy and I staggered back, looked at each other, and then saw Al lying on the ground. We helped him get up. Men were running over and asking if anyone was hurt. We asked Al what knocked him down, and he said, "I didn't fall down." We had to take off his coat and show him the mud on the back of it before he would believe that he had been down. Nothing struck him – it was the shock wave from the blast that knocked him off his feet. I was sick and later realized I was sore. We passed blood for a day or two, and at sickbay the doctor told us this was a common result of being close to this type of explosion.

At the time we assumed that there was some kind of malfunction occured. In fact, it was due to overloading the plane. Because this happened shortly after we had started flying missions, we didn't realize the threat to us. We too, were flying an overloaded B-17.

We learned later that the gross maximum weight for a B-17 was 64,000 pounds. But we regularly carried 72,000, and on one mission we took 84,000 pounds. I don't know how many B-17's crashed on takeoff before they went back to max gross weight of 64,000 pounds.

Later, an improved supercharger was developed. The old B-17G had an R-1820 engine and a supercharger that would give you 46 inches of manifold pressure. The new B-17G still had the R-1820 engines but was stronger and had superchargers that would give you not 46, but 60 inches of mercury. This plane could take off with 84,000 pounds gross easily. We never heard of one of these improved planes crashing on takeoff.

The explosion at Great Ashfield was one of the deadliest scenes we had witnessed, and it had happened on home base within close range of us. We realized that no matter where you were, whether you were in combat or not, your life could be endangered. And so it was on other occasions as we continued our tour in Europe.

Keep me safe, oh God, for I have come to you for refuge.
Psalm 16:1 NLT

MAR-27?
44

1,400 Heavies Strike 3 Big German Ports

Delivering its mightiest punch at German ports, the 8th Air Force yesterday sent more than 1,400 Fortresses and Liberators and 900 Mustangs and Thunderbolts to rake the three great Reich ports of Wilhelmshaven, Bremen and Hamburg. Submarine yards, docks, naval vessels and an oil storage depot trembled under the loads dropped by the heaviest force of bombers since Feb. 22 and the greatest combined bomber-fighter force dispatched this year by the 8th.

It was a momentous occasion for the Liberators which plastered docks and other harbor facilities in Wilhelmshaven, where the battleship Tirpitz was built. It was here that heavies of the 8th first bombed Germany, on January 27, 1943, when 53 Fortresses attacked the harbor with a loss of one and a bag of 22 Nazi fighters.

THE STARS AND STRIPES
Daily Newspaper for U.S. Armed Forces – European Theater of Operations New York, N.Y. – London, England

Bordeaux

This mission was one of supreme importance but details surrounding it were kept hidden for decades. The briefing officer explained that a ballistic missile of some new type had been launched toward the United States but had fallen short of its target landing in the Atlantic Ocean. By tracing the missile flight path backward it was determined that the origin was Bordeaux, France. Reconnaissance aircraft were sent out and came back with pictures with the launch facility. It could not be determined just what type of weapon had been used but we were sure further launches had to be prevented at all costs.

An immediate response was necessary to prevent imminent attack on US East Coast cities. The normal days spent planning each mission could not be risked, we would have only hours to prepare. A previous mission to Bordeaux proved disastrous for the fighter escorts. Many of them ran low on fuel when returning and had to land at other bases. We would have to go it alone this time.

Only one bomb group would be required, but they would have to be deadly and sure. Considering the critical nature of this mission Colonel Vandevanter made the decision to assign this special mission to the 385th Bomb Group.

Bordeaux was about as far away as a B-17 could go even if it flew straight there and back. That meant we did not have the luxury to fly around fighter bases or heavy flak areas. They would be able to hit us going in, and the same fighters could refuel and reload guns and catch us going home. We could count on lots of fighter attacks and that would keep our guns busy defending ourselves.

It didn't take a military genius to see that we were in for a big challenge. I remember Bill Clark and me presenting the suggestion that we tightly limit our shooting to conserve ammunition. Other gunners in the 550th Squadron had been thinking about the same idea. So we all got together on this strategy and promised not to shoot except at close targets or in very dangerous situations. Everyone agreed that this would be our only hope. If we ran out of ammo, the fighters could come as close as they wanted and we would be sitting ducks.

Base Commander Colonel Vandevanter said the first P-38 observation plane reported that the 385th had reached the enemy coast and had already encountered enemy fighters. His next report: we had successfully hit the target, even with a small group of enemy fighters dogging the B-17's still shooting up the formation.

At this point in the war the Germans had few fighters left. Since they had not been able to stop the bombing of the launching facility, there was no reason left for them to risk fighters and planes. Knowing that the B-17's couldn't carry enough ammunition or fuel for a long flight, they must have decided that we were no longer a threat. Whatever the reason, they discontinued their attack. Unfortunately, the P-38 observation planes had broken away shortly before this time and were returning to England.

Meanwhile at the base, Colonel Vandevanter was receiving the final report from the P-38 observation planes, who didn't know that the enemy had stopped attacking. They reported that we were just past halfway home and German fighters were still in pursuit. They also reported that it didn't appear that there was any opposition from the B-17's. The colonel feared that we were out of ammo and the enemy fighters would have no resistance.

We never ran out of fuel, and though most of us had bullet holes, we didn't lose a single airplane. For the guys that didn't fly this mission, it must not have been noteworthy. So many other missions received a lot more press and involved more bomb groups. But for us it was quite a memorable mission that eliminated a major threat without any losses of men or aircraft.

During interrogation Colonel Vandevanter met with us and shared his concern. He said that from the briefing that morning everyone knew it was going to be a very dangerous mission, and when the observation team reported the events, he had feared the worst. He expressed how pleased he was that the men were all safe and that the mission was a success.

EDITOR'S NOTE: In 1940 Germany had been developing a trans-oceanic ballistic missile designated the A9/A10. Development of this was shelved in 1942 when Hitler ordered all production efforts devoted to the V2 missile. Wernher Von Braun continued secret development under the designation A4b (a variant of the V2). Development of the A9/A10 resumed in 1944 under the code name Projekt Amerika.

Something was launched from Bordeaux in January of 1944. Aimed at the east coast of the United States, it failed to reach its intended target. The type of weapon is unknown, only the launch facility was found. Photographs taken by the USAAF showed the launch facility was destroyed. After that date, there were no further launchings. Five months later the allies landed at Normandy.

References:

http://www.ww2guide.com/vweapon.shtml

http://english.pravda.ru/main/2002/10/03/37680_.html

http://www.astronautix.com/lvs/a9a10.htm

Nazi plan to bomb New York   VHS/CD : The History Channel

Advanced Research:

http://www.nsa.gov/public/publi00004.cfm (#NR981)

http://www.nasm.si.edu/research/dsh/peenintro.html

Monday, Feb. 7, 1944

Luftwaffe's Airfields For Invasion Defense Battered by Heavies

Bombers, Out 9th Time in 10 Days, Pound French 'Dromes and Secret Targets

American and Allied air fleets smashed Luftwaffe airfields deep in France and pounded secret targets along the coast in daylight yesterday as the U.S. heavy bombers carried the war's most intensive bombing assault to nine raids in ten days.

While Fortresses and Liberators were giving the Luftwaffe's invasion defense airfields their second battering in two days, almost endless relays of other warplanes shuttled across the Channel in daylong sweeps against military installations on the French coast. Some heavy bombers also hit the secret targets which may be emplacements for Hitler's rocket guns.

From yesterday's American attacks, four heavy bombers and four fighters were reported missing. U.S. fighters claimed 13 enemy aircraft in scattered dogfights, and the bomber gunners claimed four.

The heavy bombers struck devastating blows at Nazi airdromes and depots at Evreux-Fauville, St. Andre de l'Eure, Caen, Chateaudun and St. Aubin, adding to the destruction left by Saturday's heavy daylight assault on six German-held fields in central France. At least 37 Nazi planes were reported destroyed on the ground in Saturday's blows at Chateaudun, Avord, Bricy, Tours, Chateaurous-la-Martiniere and Villacoublay, near Paris.

The Saturday attacks cost two heavy bombers and two U.S. fighters, while bomber gunners claimed four enemy planes and the fighters, six.

The weekend daylight attacks, which brought the long offensive to a peak, began with an assault in force on Frankfurt, in Germany, Friday. Twenty-one heavy bombers were reported missing and one of the escorting USAAF fighters, while bomber gunners claimed four enemy planes and the fighters eight.

THE STARS AND STRIPES
Daily Newspaper for U.S. Armed Forces – European Theater of Operations – New York, N.Y. – London, England

What can we say about such wonderful things as these?
If God is for us, who can ever be against us?
Romans 8:31 NLT

No Greater Love

February 20, 1944 – Targeting Tutow, we encountered fairly heavy flak and few fighters. The challenge that day had been the conservation of fuel since this was a ten-hour mission. We had successfully hit our target and, with the mission behind us, we made our way over to the North Sea.

A few enemy fighters still dogged the cripples. Some planes had one engine feathered, which meant they were running out of fuel. This could potentially be a death sentence if something more critical didn't take them down first. If the battered aircraft could make it out to sea, the English Rescue teams would pick up the soldiers.

These rescuers were absolutely fearless in the face of coastal gunfire, fighter planes, and the ever threatening North Sea. They never failed to retrieve surviving crewmen after a Flying Fortress was ditched at sea.

Far ahead of us just such a plane and its crew had gone down in the dark waters. Once a crew bails out or otherwise abandons their plane, the Geneva Convention forbids any further attack, but some Germans ignored this agreement.

The men were struggling to get into their rafts when the enemy plane which had ended their flight made a sharp turn. As the enemy maneuvered into position to shoot the crew in their rafts, the anticipation of their impending doom was brief but horrific just the same.

We were an unwilling audience watching what we perceived to be a hopeless plight as the B-17 sank. The Fortress took a nosedive into the North Sea, pulling the tail up out of the water. The tail gunner had stayed at his guns and, miraculously, he was still alive. As the enemy fighter came in a little closer, the tail guns of the battered B-17 blazed a long burst of .50 caliber shells at the Messerschmitt.

Though the B-17 had long since lost its power, these guns were hand held and didn't require electric motors to move. The enemy plane was about four or five-hundred yards away when it was riddled with bullets. The Messerschmitt literally exploded before he was able to fire his guns.

This brave tail gunner with a calm spirit and steady hands saved his crew while he sacrificed his own life. I later heard that he had been awarded the Congressional Medal of Honor. The medal was certainly warranted, but I believe that it gave no consolation to the family he left behind.

After witnessing this bittersweet victory, we landed at Great Ashfield, England, where we would repeat the routine of interrogation, chow, and hopefully get some rest. It was against human nature to shake off a mission's tragedies, especially ones like today's. But there would be another day and another mission that would require everything we had. We couldn't be prepared for the next mission if we didn't let go of the last. It was only possible by God's grace, which gave us the spirit and the strength to go on.

This is my commandment, that ye love one another, as I have loved you. Greater love hath no man than this, that a man lay down his life for his friends.
John 15:12-13 KJV

Breathing Fire

On one mission in the winter of 1944, enemy fire had left us with serious battle damage. The B-17's hydraulic system took the worst of it. There was hydraulic fluid all over the floor and the pressure gauge fell to zero.

Now, the hydraulic pump had no fuse or manual switch with which to shut it off. Because it had lost all of the fluid, the pump couldn't cool itself. And without fluid there was nothing to trigger the built-in pressure switch, which was designed to shut off the pump.

I knew the motor and the pump were bound to burn up even though it was very cold. The pump's plug was safety wired. It should have had small copper wire (.0031) but instead it was wired with no. 41 stainless steel, and I had no tools to work with.

I tried to tear the lead wire off but couldn't break it. About this time I saw a red glow and some sparks. That's when the vapors from the hydraulic fuel exploded and the cockpit was engulfed in flames. I grabbed the fire extinguisher, pulled the safety loose, and sent a stream shooting out over the fire. I kept spraying the pump and motor, and with the benefit of wind blowing hard through the aircraft, I thought I had the upper hand.

I was using a carbon-tetrachloride extinguisher – carbon-tet, we called it. When this chemical hits the fire it makes phosgene gas – a very toxic and deadly gas.

We had been flying below 10,000 feet, so there had been no need for us to use our oxygen masks. When the fire broke out, everyone else put on their masks. I had to act so quickly in the crisis that I hadn't had a chance to get my mask. All this time I had been holding my breath.

Unable to hold my breath any longer, I gasped, inhaling the caustic fumes. I remember that it felt like I had breathed fire into my lungs! The pain was so great that I passed out. Paul Starr put my mask over my face and turned the oxygen on and I came to. It was like waking up in hell.

The first clear thought that came to me was that it's going to explode again! I put the rest of the carbon-tet on the motor and pump to cool them. Then, with all my strength, I ripped the wires off! Back in my turret I sat down, and I think I remember crying. Paul had saved my life without any doubt.

Even though I had very little strength for several days, I continued to fly every mission. There was some permanent damage to my lungs, but I never claimed any disability. I am grateful for having had the opportunity to serve my country. I believe I may have even lived longer because of the training and the hard living we experienced.

The grave wrapped its ropes around me;
death itself stared me in the face.
But in my distress I cried out to the Lord;
yes, I prayed to my God for help.
He heard me from his sanctuary;
my cry reached his ears.
Psalm 18:5-6 NLT

Shoot-Out over the North Sea

February 24, 1944 – This was my twelfth mission, and we were being sent to Rostock, Germany. We hit the target with great success. The pilots broke formation and headed for England. Flying as individual aircraft eliminated the need for constantly adjusting speed and therefore conserved fuel.

We had made it out over the North Sea when I noticed a Messerschmitt 110 at 3 o'clock level with us. He was out of range for a .50 caliber but flying slow to keep even with us. I noted that this 110 had rockets under its wings. These were guided rockets, and some Luftwaffe fighters were experienced enough to put them right through a B-17's waist window. A hit with one of these rockets always took the Fortress down.

This ME pilot seemed to be waiting for something as he steadily slipped in closer. He was now about 1200 yards out, according to my range-finder. I'm sure the fighter was aware that our guns had a maximum reach of approximately 1000 yards and could only be considered dependable at 600 yards or less. Then it struck me: he was getting a kick out of toying with us! He had little to fear since he could fire the rocket from a great distance and then guide it to his target.

Even though it seemed that any effort would be futile, I opened fire at just under 1200 yards. The ME just kept sliding in closer, apparently planning to attack at about 1000 yards. I had plenty of ammunition left and nothing to lose, so I steadied my guns, took good time to aim, and began firing again. Now the fighter was within about 800 yards of us. I can't begin to describe the intensity of that moment as I expected him to turn toward us any second and fire the deadly rockets. The reason he didn't would soon be clear.

The fighter began to turn alright, nose-down, dropping out of my view and diving straight into the North Sea. I had fired over 200 rounds in short, well-aimed bursts. One bullet may have hit the pilot. Airmen from other B-17's who had tracked him all the way down reported that an engine was afire. I was unable to see this since he had gone below my sights. Officers from three different crews confirmed the kill, and as I was the only one firing his guns, I was credited with this one.

Much was made of the fact that the enemy fighter carried two guided missiles but had been prevented from firing either of them. I was awarded the Distinguished Flying Cross. This was a very humbling experience. Any experienced .50 caliber gunner knows that this plane was too far away for the shots to be accurate. The Lord blessed my efforts anyway and gave me that little victory. We had avoided disaster again and survived to fly another day.

If the righteous are rewarded here on earth, how much more true
that the wicked and the sinner will get what they deserve!
Proverbs 11:31 NLT

USAAF Photo personally presented to Oral F. Lindsey

SERGEANT LINDSEY.

Sergeant Holds DFC, Air Medal

STAMFORD, May 28 (Spl.) — Having completed 25 combat missions and destroyed one German plane, a twin-engine Messerschmitt-110 fighter, Tech. Sgt. Orel F. Lindsey holds the DFC and Air Medal with four clusters and hopes to come home soon.

He is the son of Mr. and Mrs. J. F. Lindsey of Route 2, Stamford, and has been ovrseas since November. He served in England as engineer and top turret gunner of a Flying Fortress called Barbara B.

Lindsey's missions included attacks on Berlin, Augsburg, Frankfurt, Muenster, Bremen, Brunswick, Rostock, Warnemuende and Diepholz.

THE STARS AND STRIPES
Daily Newspaper for U.S. Armed Forces – European Theater of Operations New York, N.Y. – London, England

ORAL LINDSEY

Continued from page 1

rial targets in Germany and Nazi-occupied Europe.

Sgt. Lindsey, son of Mr. and and Mrs. J. F. Lindsey of Route 2, Stamford, has also received the Air Medal with four Oak Leaf Clusters.

While defending his Fortress and crew from enemy fighter attack, the Texas gunner has been credited with destruction of a Messerschmitt 110, enemy twin-engine fighter plane.

"That Me went straight down like a quail shot stone dead," he said. "He was coming in on our tail when I caught the fellow in my sights and poured the ammunition into him. One engine caught fire and down he went." The formation in which Sgt. Lindsey was flying was under fighter attack at intervals for nearly two hours that day, but successfully bombed military installations in northeastern Germany.

Fighters were not the only danger which the Texas flier faced. "Flak frightened me as much as anything else," he stated. "Once over Augsburg a piece of flak ripped through the nose of our ship, shattered a brace under the pilot's seat and finally slammed into me from the rear. If that brace had not been where it was, I probably wouldn't be alive to tell about it.

The Texan has flown on missions to such targets as the marshalling yards of Frankfurt and Munster, ship yards at Bremen, aircraft factories and component parts plants at Brunswick, Augsburg and Diepholz, industrial targets in Munich, Rostock and Warnemunde, and ball-bearing plants at Berlin.

Sgt. Lindsey entered the AAF in October 1942, attending air mechanics school at Sheppard Field, Texas, specialist mechanic school at Seattle, Wash., and aerial gunnery school at Wendover Field, Utah, before entering training for overseas service on Flying Fortresses.

Distinguished Flying Cross

USAAF – AIR MEDAL

War's Greatest Tragedy

March 3, 1944 – Our outfit, the 385th Bomb Group, and the rest of the Third Division were being sent to Berlin. The First Division had left before us and had already bombed Berlin. While those bomber groups were making their way home, a massive cloud cover had been quickly developing and rose to 50,000 feet over Germany. As far as I knew, there was no change in orders as a result of this weather development. Everything was going according to the plan, or so everyone thought.

Our formation was clipping along at 160 mph, making our way through the dense clouds. Then, without warning, our whole world was scrambled. Headed straight toward us through the murky skies appeared the Fortresses of the First Division.

Imagine the horror of 126 planes meeting another division of planes head-on, both flying at 160 mph air speed! It was the unthinkable, yet it was clearly a reality. My heart sank and fear swept over me as I looked on from a front row seat. It appeared to me that at least five B-17's hit five other ships head-on. Suddenly it was raining airplanes. What had been an orderly formation of planes with a specific target became chaos as each pilot sought out his own path. It was all over in a matter of seconds.

The combined speed for the two divisions was 320 miles per hour. Flying just over five miles per minute, a ship covers a mile in less than twelve seconds – just long enough for the pilots to see each other's planes, but not enough time to avoid the disaster. It truly was a miracle that many more B-17's weren't lost. Throughout the collisions I never saw a parachute, but the clouds beneath us would have obscured them from view.

The First Division had made it outside the cloud cover when the mission was recalled. Our division had to turn around and then head for clearer skies to re-form. No one talked about it, and I dared not asked questions of those in authority. I never heard an explanation given, and as far as I know, this incident was never mentioned in our 385th history.

FORMATION VAPOR TRAILS
USAAF Photo – Declassified

Don't be afraid, for I am with you.
Do not be dismayed, for I am your God. I will strengthen you.
I will help you. I will uphold you with my victorious right hand.
Isaiah 41:10 NLT

Missing Blast Tubes

We had been assigned a new airplane to replace our good old Barbara B that had been shot down, killing all crew members. Leach and I were left to prepare this new plane for combat. We called all the necessary specialists – armament, electrical, and any others who were required to prepare the new ship for combat.

Everything was in order except that armament informed me that there were no blast tubes in supply. The Browning .50 caliber has a terrible breath as anyone will tell you if they've had it blown in their face. The blast tube is a strong piece of steel pipe that fits over the barrel jacket and is cut away at the top to deflect the high pressure gas upward. Noise from the blast is directed up and away as well.

We looked everywhere imaginable but failed to find any blast tubes. This was a critical item, but certainly not enough to ground the flight. All systems were checked and the plane was now ready for combat.

On this plane's first mission we hadn't even reached the target when I spotted some dots straight ahead. I was assigned to guarding the front of the formation, and my guns were almost aligned with the tiny specks. It was a small group of Messerschmitts on a sneak frontal attack. On such an attack you have about a four-second window in which the enemy can be shot at with any great success. I was ready for them with proper settings on the computing sight. They came in like a streak of lightening! I held my guns steady and started firing when the fighters were out about 800 yards. At about 400 yards, they broke away.

Not one went down, but their attack was certainly foiled. We had survived this enemy attack, but you can never let your guard down. I had learned that there was no such thing as a "safe zone."

Captain Clark was screaming at me over the intercom, but I didn't even respond. There wasn't time. Another ME 109 was coming straight for our airplane, and I gave him the same greeting I gave his buddies. He had as good of an aim as I did; we both missed each other!

It looked like that was the last of them for the moment, so I climbed down out of the turret to see what the shouting was about. I saw Clark was madder than an old wet hen. Then, looking up, I saw that one of the overhead windows was gone. The blast from the .50 caliber gun had blown the Plexiglas® window out. It was a forceful blow.

I knew the percussion was bad, but I never realized it was capable of that kind of damage. Along with some colorful names embellished with descriptive adjectives, he informed me that it cracked his helmet liner and, he believed, his skull!

I guess he wasn't impressed with my aim. He said nothing about the fact that I had fended off the enemy. It probably had something to do with the splitting headache that I had given him. It was never again necessary to fire directly over the pilot's canopy on that mission or any other. There were no other significant encounters this trip.

When we returned to base, I wasted no time in trying to redeem myself. The pressure was on. I began my search again, and this time found a plane that was grounded. I didn't see any of the ground crew, so I quickly climbed onto the plane and confiscated a set of blast tubes. Clark wasn't my best friend for a long time, but he finally forgave me.

Fear of the Lord teaches a person to be wise;
humility precedes honor.
Proverbs 15:33 NLT

The Whole Nine Yards

We had just returned from a mission and were unloading the plane. Every crew went through this process at the end of each mission. It was supposed to be the usual routine before going to interrogation. We were safely back on base but physically worn and mentally frazzled. All we could think about was getting these tasks out of the way so we could go to chow and then hit the sack.

Once the plane landed and the ground crew chocked the wheels, the guns were removed from their turrets and the rest of our heavy clothes and gear would be put into bags. Once the crew and their gear were loaded onto a truck, we were driven to the armament shack where we dropped off the guns for cleaning. The next stop would be the parachute shop, which was next to the locker room. Here the parachutes were checked in and the men would then go to the locker room to change into their fatigues.

Everything was going fine. The guns had been dropped off and we were being driven to the parachute shop. On the jaunt across the airfield, we were wearing our parachutes to free our hands for carrying bags.

The truck had just come to a stop and the men were jumping out. With a duffel bag in one hand and B-Bag in the other, I stood up and jumped out of the back of the truck. As I made the four-foot drop, my D-ring got caught on the tailgate of the truck and twenty-four feet of pure white (spring loaded) nylon shot out into the air, billowing out over the black English mud! I felt like an idiot.

It wasn't funny to me, but everyone else was having a heyday. When they were able to stop laughing, they helped me gather my dirty canopy and carry it to the chute shop just a few yards away.

I expected to catch heck from the guys in the parachute shop, but everyone was very considerate. I think I felt worse about the blunder than if I had been chewed out for the mishap.

> *I waited patiently for the Lord to help me,*
> *and he turned to me and heard my cry.*
> *He lifted me out of the pit of despair,*
> *out of the mud and the mire.*
> *He set my feet on solid ground*
> *and steadied me as I walked along.*
> *Psalm 40:1-2 NLT*

Midnight Requisitioning

A group of us guys were just hanging out at the barracks and the subject of food came up. Someone said, "I haven't tasted jelly since I left the states." Now, we knew that the mess hall got jelly, but the cooks either sold it or gave it to their girlfriends. Maybe they just ate it. Whatever the case, we certainly never got any.

After some deliberation, four of us agreed to raid the mess hall and get us some real food, especially jelly. We called it Midnight Requisitioning. In any other situation it might have been called stealing. The plan was simple if nothing else. One or two would cause trouble in the dining hall. We were sure that all the cooks and KP's would leave the kitchen to watch the fight. While they were distracted, the rest of us would raid the pantry.

I decided I was a better thief than a fighter, so Eddie and I planned to raid the store. Roy was the toughest, so he and another guy started a fist fight near the entry door (for a quick get-away). We went into the mess hall just ahead of the other guys. We hung around close to the doorway at the back where we weren't allowed. As soon as all the cooks piled out of the kitchen, we darted in.

You wouldn't believe the treasures we found! We loaded up with 18-inch loaves of fresh bread, the kind that has a hard crust but is great on the inside. We found canned milk and a 2-lb can of coffee. And yes, we did get jelly – grape jelly to be exact, along with two pounds of butter. We scrambled out the back, putting as much of the booty into the basket on my bicycle as possible. Eddie carried the rest.

To better our chances, we avoided all bike trails. Plowing through the dark woods, Eddie and I were running over sticks, rocks and through big holes, hitting limbs and occasionally a tree!

At the barracks the guys greeted us like heroes. Although Eddie and I had scratches all over and Roy was beaten up some, we had all made it back safely. Roy complained, "Ole Tex and Eddie were just standing up there watching me get the tar beat out of me." All of the guys started laughing, but I know he didn't see the humor in it.

In the sweeping raid we had also scooped up a couple of jars of peanut butter and a can of cocoa. We made sandwiches while the coffee perked on the little heater in our barracks. Boy, did we have ourselves a feast. There was much more than the guys could eat, so we stashed the rest. It's amazing how well you sleep when your belly is full. As far as I know none of this was ever mentioned to those guys that had been out that night. If any of you guys are reading this now, I offer my sincere apologies.

For all have sinned; all fall short of God's glorious standard.
Yet now God in his gracious kindness declares us not guilty.
He has done this through Christ Jesus,
who has freed us by taking our sins.
Romans 3:23-24 NLT

Coal Heater & Sometimes Cook Stove
Photo from "Target: Germany" a USAAF Publication Printed
by The Sun Engraving Co., Ltd., London and Watford

School of Hard Knocks

Collier, a young recruit in our barracks, had come from a very wealthy family and was truly doing his best to survive under the harsh conditions of war. He was well- educated and well-groomed, but he didn't have any experience out in the world. This definitely left him at a disadvantage in our current environment. He never seemed to know what to do.

The military isn't able to teach a man everything he needs to know to survive in wartime. Sometimes common sense is the only tool he has. My father appreciated the observation that common sense isn't common. He passed that truth along to me while I was still a child. As an adult I decided that some people just do not have the logic it takes to have common sense. I also believed that it took some life experience and maturity to have a lot of common sense.

Thinking about experience and common sense reminds me of the first encounter I had with this young man. During a bombing raid I jumped behind a telephone pole – not much of a shield, but it was the only cover I could find. In the next split second, this kid plowed into me, knocking me right out into the open. Fortunately, neither of us was injured.

As we were walking away I said, "Man, don't ever push me out in the open like that!"

He said, "I'm sorry, Sarge. I didn't know what to do."

I explained to him that next time he'd better just find his place behind me, not try to take mine!

On another occasion, after we were well asleep, Collier came stumbling into the barracks and woke me up. He said, "Sarge, sorry to wake you, but I'm starvin' to death. Have you got anything to eat?"

What a coincidence. This was the same night we had raided the mess hall. I couldn't say no. This kid was like a fish out of water, and he was drunk to boot. I asked him, "What'd you want?"

The kid said, "I'll eat anything from shoe leather on."

I told him to give me a few minutes and I'd see what I could come up with. I found the coffee pot and poured in some canned milk with a little water. As I set it on the heater to warm up I asked, "How does hot cocoa sound?"

He said, "Sarge, you wouldn't kid me? I know you usually have a little something tucked away, but I can't believe this."

We didn't take any sugar that night in the raid, because we could get sugar cubes. They were rationed, but available. I didn't use sugar in my coffee, so I always saved mine. Fortunately for him, I still had sugar cubes for his cocoa. Fixed up with a cup of hot cocoa and a chunk of bread, he quit thinking about starving and slept like a log.

There were other times when Collier needed somebody to give him a hand. He was a willing student and never expected any special treatment because of his background. Collier's only downfall was his youth. I think he was only eighteen or nineteen when he arrived in England. We all have to get experience somewhere, and I think God put him there so I could take him in under my wing.

How precious is your unfailing love, oh God!
All humanity finds shelter in the shadow of your wings.
Psalm 36:7   NLT

Fire and Ice

Another less funny thing happened to me on the return from a mission to Munich. It had been a nearly routine day. We hit our target and were now about an hour into our return trip to base. The plane had taken some hits from fighter machine guns, but all seemed to be going well. It was a long mission and we had burned a lot of fuel, but we still had enough to make it home.

We had not seen any more fighters. Though from my position in the top turret it appeared we were in safe territory, I continued to keep a lookout. Then, for no apparent reason that I can remember, I looked down. I was horrified to see a little trickle of flame coming up my pant leg. My flight suit was on fire! An electrical short in my heated suit had started the fire. There was no option but to unplug the suit.

It was very cold, minus 65 degrees, with wind blowing through the old B-17 from every crack and opening. There was no heat and the wind was whipping my pant legs like a West Texas sandstorm. Closing the bulkhead doors to the bomb bay helped a little.

Clark said, "I guess I don't have to tell you how serious this is." He reminded me that according to official reports, the time it took for a man to freeze to death was about thirty minutes, give or take a few. It was nearly four hours until let down.

Many B-17s had heated sleeping bags for emergencies, but not this one. I stood up and exercised to help keep up circulation. I stood out of the wind as best I could, but soon I began to weaken and even hallucinate. Clark was constantly talking to me and encouraging me to hang on. In time I quit responding to him. He left his seat and tried rousing my consciousness, but I was so delirious all I wanted to do was fall asleep. That's when he slapped me! I snapped back, alright. I was fighting mad and would have struck a return blow, but I was too numb.

He said, "Listen, Tex! I'm trying to save your life!" Of course I realized that as soon as I returned to my wits. With my pilot's determination and a lot of guts, I managed the longest three hours of my life. Finally, Clark told the group leader that we were falling out of formation. He said, "My flight engineer's freezing to death and I'm taken her down."

After what seemed to be an eternity we arrived safely at Great Ashfield. Once we had unloaded and were at our lockers, Roy and Al took my flying clothes off and dressed me like a paralytic. I couldn't move my arms or legs, but I was alive!

When a crew returned home and went into debriefing, there would always be coffee and whiskey available to them. They were actually combat rations. Each man was allotted a maximum of two shots of whiskey – smooth Kentucky sippin' whiskey, to be exact. As you entered the room there was a table where coffee was being served, and across the room from that was the bar. It was usually attended by a young lady and always with an officer on guard. Being half-frozen, I wasn't thinking about having coffee as usual. I eagerly took two shots of whiskey and promptly fell asleep in my chair.

They could bust you for sleeping through interrogation, but they never bothered me. I supposed that with Clark's report they figured the Air Corp was lucky to have me back. For three hours I had survived in conditions where it had been believed a man could only make it thirty minutes.

Homer Bigart, war correspondent of The Writing 69th
and winner of two Pulitzer Prizes,
wrote this after a mission over Germany:

"A mission to Germany is a nasty experience. Apart from the very real danger to life and limb, there is the acute discomfort of enduring sub-zero temperatures for hours at a stretch and taking air through an oxygen mask. The altitude can affect your sinews, your kidneys, even the fillings of your teeth. You are very tired when you return. If you are a delayed-reaction type, you are likely to feel slightly under par for a couple of days. I must be crazy, but I should like to go again."

(Quote From The Writing 69th website
sponsored by Green Harbor Publications.)
www.greenharbor.com/wr69/Biographies.html

"I will give you back your health and heal your wounds,"
says the Lord.
Jeremiah 30:17a NLT

Dogfight

While I can't place the date or even which target we hit, I do remember vividly a deadly encounter with the enemy. We were leaving the German coast and headed for England. Our crew had all but used up the last of their ammunition during the battle, and because it had been such a long trip, all the B-17's were running low on fuel. The formation spread out so everyone could fly independently. This way the pilots were able to conserve gasoline. We were holding our own, but our day wasn't over yet.

A lone fighter picked us out and made a pass from our right wing at three o'clock. I was very low on ammo and only gave him a short burst. He came all the way across us, passing over my turret. Then he whipped around and at short range opened up with his 20 millimeters. Unable to follow him with the turret, I told Clark to drop quickly, which he did. The shells all went over us.

If we did the same thing again, the enemy pilot would be warned of our strategy and surely would hit us next time. Sure enough, he circled back around, positioning his plane to repeat the stunt that had almost netted him a solid hit.

I quickly thought of another strategy and told Clark. He agreed that it might work and waited for my signal. I turned my turret around with my back to the incoming fighter, waiting for him to play right into our hands. Looking over my shoulder, I saw the Messerschmitt's guns light up and yelled, "Now!" Bill dropped about forty feet and left my heart up there.

We were set up now and just hoping that he would follow through with the same maneuver as before. My guns would be right on him. I was just praying that he wouldn't notice my position until it was too late.

As we anticipated, the fighter came over us and then turned the nimble Messerschmitt on a dime. Suddenly, he was square in my reticules! I didn't check the range or anything. He was so close I just put the horizontal wire on the pilot about midway of the wire and squeezed the trigger on my .50 calibers. It was only a short burst, but all my cartridges were "hanging up," about ten left on one side and less on the other. I had hit the Messerschmitt, and the fighter's canopy blew off!

He made a beautiful recovery. The fighter was already flying slower than normal in order to move around us. When the canopy blew off and that blast of air hit him, he acted quickly. Of course, I was hoping to see a chute as he bailed out, but no such luck. This fighter pilot was very capable, and there was apparently no other damage to his plane. He put the ME 109 in a steep climb, throttle back, and headed for home. It was an honorable duel, and we had both survived to try each other again another day.

Someone said, "That's a great trick if you have the guts to turn your back on four 20mm cannons."

I said, "But by tomorrow it will be an old trick. Next time around the pilot will be looking to see if your guns are pointing at him or not. I wouldn't try it again for anything."

I considered this mission to be one of the most successful as we had narrowly escaped a fatal encounter with the enemy. Sure, some of us might have been able to bail out on the way down – that is, if our ship didn't explode. But no one wanted to think about the possibilities.

My enemies turn away in retreat;
they are overthrown and destroyed before you.
Psalm 9:3 NLT

Over 850 Forts, Libs Set Capital Aflame In Great Fire Raid

Smoke Visible 100 Miles After Second Major Day Attack; Fierce Air Battles Deepen Gash in the Luftwaffe

THE STARS AND STRIPES
Daily Newspaper for U.S. Armed Forces – European Theater of Operations New York, N.Y. – London, England

Berlin got its second major daylight bombing yesterday. A force of American Flying Fortresses and Liberators estimated at more than 850 strong dropped more than 350,000 incendiary bombs and 10,000 high-explosive bombs on the German capital, and returning airmen said the smoke billowing from the burning ruins could be seen 100 miles away.

Thirty-eight American bombers and 16 fighters were lost in the operations according to an announcement from U.S. Strategic Air Forces headquarter just before midnight. U.S. fighters claimed 83 enemy aircraft destroyed; bombers crews' claims have not tabulated.

The attack, third by American forces on Berlin in four days, was probably the biggest daylight incendiary raid in history, far surpassing the German attempt to set London afire on Sept. 15, 1940, at the start of the London blitz.

A preliminary report from headquarters shortly before midnight said that the ball bearing plant at Erkner, 15 miles southeast of the heart of the city, was heavily hit and that "other targets in the area also were bombed successfully."

The Erkner plant produces half the minimum requirements in ball bearings needed by the Luftwaffe. It is second in importance only to Schweinfurt and Stuttgart, both heavily damaged by the USSTAF and RAF.

Furious air battles, possibly matching those of the Monday raid on the capital, raged across Germany from the time the bombers passed Hanover, 150 miles from the capital, shortly after noon until they emerged on the homeward flight.

Mustang pilots returning early in the afternoon said that Berlin's defenses were just as fierce and determined as in the first major assault on the city. The Monday operation cost the American forces 68 bombers and 11 fighters and the Luftwaffe 176 fighters, according to official figures at U.S. headquarters.

Berlin radio said last night more than 60 U.S. bombers were shot down.

While most bomber formations reported resistance generally less than Monday, one combat wing hit strong formations of German fighters estimated at between 100 and 200.

The precision assault in nearly cloudless skies was aimed at industrial targets still standing after the RAF's 15 night attacks, in which approximately 27,000 tons of bombs were hurled onto the city.

The battle was fought in an almost cloudless sky, with visibility marred only by the myriad puffs of ack-ack fire thrown up by German guns, the airmen said. The flak was so heavy, they added, that it appeared obvious the Germans had brought in new defenses since the Monday raid.

BERLIN ARTICLE

Replacement Crews

Around the first of April we got three new crews to replace recent losses. It was a very common thing as planes were lost on almost every mission. Usually, the new crews would be eager to learn all they could about the high altitude, the cold, and any survival tips that an experienced combat soldier could give. This new bunch was different. They made fun of how worn-out and haggard everyone was. A flight engineer laughed and said, "You look sorry to me. If you can make it here, I should have a real easy time of it."

They made their first mission to Chartres, France, a mere milk run. Their second one was a division recall – another milk run of three hours and thirty minutes flying time. Back at Great Ashfield the same flight engineer told me, "It's easier than I thought."

On the thirteenth of April we went to Augsburg, Germany. Before we took off, I saw this flight engineer and told him that after he made a mission to Augsburg, he could say he had flown a combat mission. I said, "You haven't flown one yet."

He said, "I'll do better than you."

It was like all trips to that area. The flak was heavy and the fighters were skilled. The German fighters fought right through their own anti-aircraft fire. We lost several airplanes over the target, and others were badly damaged.

When we landed back at Great Ashfield, England, we heard that all three of the new crews were lost. The guys that had criticized us and had been so arrogant were now gone along with the rest of their crew members. I did not appreciate *some* of these men, and

I had even been mad about their hateful remarks. But that was the last thing on my mind now. Many young lives had been taken, and many families would be filled with grief.

Losing so many young men at one time was devastating. Those men were from the barracks right behind ours, so we had seen them every day. I decided to walk over and take a look into the barracks, hoping to talk to some of the guys from another crew, but I found only military personnel gathering the soldiers' personal things. I learned that the new guys were the only men housed in that barracks.

That same night, the young recruit, Collier, and I were alone in our barracks. Everyone else had gone to the NCO Club, Red Cross, a movie, or somewhere. It was after dark but very early in the evening when the siren was sounded. Collier and I were in our bunks, but quickly jumped to our feet at the sound of a German bomb exploding very near us. A second later, another bomb hit much closer.

I knew the enemy carried three bombs, and as my mind raced, it seemed to me that the next one would be in our barracks. Sure enough, just as the world blew up, we hit the floor. Every door and window was blown open or blown off. Fortunately, our pride was the only thing wounded.

Collier said, "Sarge, why did you hit me?"

I said, "I didn't hit you."

He said, "I saw you. You just knocked me down, and I don't know why!"

Then I realized that, in fact, I had *helped* him to the floor.

It might not have been necessary, but my survival instincts kicked in, and I guess I just took him with me. I knew at the very least there would be debris flying everywhere, and I was getting out of the way.

The last bomb had hit in the middle of the barracks just behind us and went deep in the ground before exploding. This kept us from getting any of the direct concussion, but it sure opened up the barracks and our ears.

I apologized to Collier, telling him that I never knew I hit him, and we both laughed. It did seem comical because he was much bigger than me and a tough kid.

The humor didn't linger long. We were thinking about the crews that didn't make it home. If those men had been in their barracks that night, they surely would have been killed. Had I been superstitious, that barracks and the demise of its crews would have been taken as proof of a curse.

> *True humility and fear of the Lord*
> *lead to riches, honor, and long life.*
> *Proverbs 22:4 NLT*

Southport Merseyside

The Augsburg target made us twenty-six missions and we hadn't been given a break yet. Normally a crew would be scheduled for a trip to the rest home on about their fifteenth mission. Everyone looked forward to this mid-tour vacation, and we were way overdue.

We were rushed off by train and taken to the Palace Hotel at Southport, England. We arrived before suppertime that afternoon – right about time for "High Tea," if I recall correctly. I could hear music coming from the lobby, so I walked in and saw a lady playing the piano. The troops were mesmerized by this young lady's poise and beauty.

Being the bashful and modest American that I was, I walked up to her in the middle of the tune and asked her for a date. She laughed at me while the other men just stood back with their mouths gaping open. She pushed the piano bench over, making room for me to sit down and asked, "Do you mind if I finish this?" I have to say that was the longest concerto ever played. Finally, she finished the piece with a great flourish, turned to me, and said "My name's Gaye Smith". That's when I introduced myself.

We went to dinner together that evening and then on to a show place where we watched a few of the acts – none of which I remember. After that evening we had almost every meal together. We had some meals at the Palace Hotel, but we went out once or twice every day, and some days even three times.

I made a point of telling her that I was a combat man and that each time we left the runway, I had no great expectations of making it back alive. There was no hope for any kind of a relationship between us. Gaye was not only beautiful but very intelligent and mature. She still wanted to continue dating, so each day when her volunteer service at the hotel was completed, we would hit the streets again.

It was great fun. The English welcomed me everywhere we went, and I found them to be the most humble and friendly people that I had ever met. Gaye was so elegant and beautiful that just her presence was a blessing.

I'm sure that I was an attraction of a different sort with my Texas accent. The locals always had a hundred questions for me about Texas, cowboys, and shoot-outs. The English would say that I talked like Jimmy Stewart and resembled him, too. Of course, no one from America would think so. All in all, it was an interesting cultural exchange.

I will never forget the first time I called on Gaye at her home. She gave me a simple address – first house on Lord Street. She said that I couldn't miss it, and I replied, "Wanna bet?" I had heard this before from the Brits. I spent a lot of time winding through the narrow streets looking for addresses.

But I didn't miss this one. I saw the first house, a cut rock mansion to me, and out front a large bronze plaque engraved – "The Smiths of Lord Street." I almost lost my courage. This could be worse than combat, I thought after surveying the situation. But I mustered all the confidence I had and was ready to face the dragon, if that was what I had waiting for me behind the huge doors.

Back in reality, I rang the doorbell and instead of a dragon or powerful lord, a sweet lady greeted me and said, "Come in." She was beautiful like Gaye, only matured. She introduced herself as Gaye's mother. I tipped my hat and then pointed to my muddy shoes. She explained that mud is always with you in England and showed me the first mat outside. After cleaning my shoes there I stepped inside and used the second mat in the entryway before stepping onto the carpet.

I never knew that carpet like that existed, let alone ever stood on any like it. It was so deep I wondered how a woman in heels could keep her balance. Mrs. Smith modestly pointed out that her husband was a ship captain and had found this piece somewhere in the Orient. She encouraged me not to fret about walking on the carpet. She said it was very durable and needed to be cleaned anyway.

It was a very pleasant experience to meet Gaye's mother. We visited for a while and then Gaye and I went out for the evening.

When you are escorting a lady like Gaye, there is always someone who's going to challenge you. Almost every time we left the hotel some guy would question me about her, as if I should share the company. These guys never considered whether she was interested in them or not – what arrogance. I would simply tell them that the lady is with me – and of her own accord. Often the guy would get mad at me and want to start trouble.

Once a lieutenant got belligerent and cursed me as we were starting to leave. I was just a tech sergeant, and he seemed to think that because he out-ranked me, that gave him some priority with Gaye. About this time my pilot, Captain Clark, walked up and said to the lieutenant, "You're lucky this boy is an enlisted man or he would tear you up. I'm an officer, so why don't you just jump on me?" The lieutenant mumbled something and walked away.

In town, two sailors made insinuating remarks about Gaye. I quickly ran toward them, and they took off. One guy lost his hat and halted immediately. I scooped it up and just stood there waiting for the sailor to approach. He couldn't go back to base without his hat. I said, "Apologize to the lady, and I'll give you your hat." He stepped forward, red-faced, and made his apology to Gaye. He seemed sincere, so I dusted off his hat and handed it to him.

All of us hated to leave the Palace Hotel when our ten-day leave was over. It seemed especially difficult for me, because it was the day I had to say goodbye to Gaye. It must have been very hard for her, too. We had grown really fond of each other, and I believed that even her mother had hopes that we would stay together. But I knew this young lady and her family were wealthy. I had nothing at the time but a job that was probably going to get me killed. Even if I made it through the war alive, I had no future befitting of her. My home was in the States, and to take her away from her homeland and family wouldn't have been right. I cared enough for Gaye that I wanted the best for her.

I never lied to Gaye or her mother about my intentions. When my missions were completed, I wrote her several times, but we did not meet again. It may seem cruel, but the war wasn't over, and I planned to return to combat if possible. Another contact and then another goodbye would be even more difficult.

The men loaded up and we were taken back to Great Ashfield. When we reported in at the 385th, Major Tesla took one look at us and said, "You men can't fly in this condition. Looks like you'll have to have a day to recover from your rest."

So there is a special rest still waiting for the people of God.
Hebrews 4:9   NLT

Bail Out or Fall Out!

March 4, 1944 – We tried again to fly our mission but the clouds were even worse, so again our division was recalled from Germany. Morale was the lowest that I had ever seen after two incomplete missions and heavy casualties. We had not had a shoot-out, let alone bombed a target during the last two missions, and yet we had been in more danger than a heated battle.

March 8, 1944 – Finally, the clouds opened and we were on our way to Berlin. Mustang P-51's escorted us on this trip. We met no fighter opposition, and flak was scarce compared to what we had encountered at Bremen. I said, "It looks like the Germans are just about beaten!"

In fact, they were almost beaten in the air, but not at all on the ground. Our ground forces would still face an almost unbeatable resistance from enemy artillery, tanks, and infantry that had the advantage of many dug-in fortresses. However, there was one thing we had been able to do for the ground fighters. We had almost taken out the Luftwaffe, and we had destroyed so much of their fuel that even good airplanes, tanks, and artillery were often abandoned.

March 11, 1944 – We flew to Munster, and on the 15th we were sent again to Brunswick.

March 16, 1944 – Our mission to Augsburg covered beautiful country but there was nothing beautiful about the battle in the skies above. This turned out to be one of the significant missions that help put an end to Goering's Luftwaffe. The US forces put up 2000 bombers to meet the challenge of everything Germany had left.

On this mission our squadron didn't have one of the more dangerous positions in formation but we still had our share of the action. We had met enemy fighters and the crew was already tired by the time we reached the target. Our ship sustained battle damage but the Flying Fortresses with their crews successfully wiped out the target over Augsburg, Germany.

Until this point in the mission we hadn't encountered any mechanical malfunctions but then everything that could possibly go wrong did go wrong.

First we lost an oxygen system. I never figured out if it was enemy fire or a mechanical malfunction that shut it down. We switched the failed turret's oxygen over to a good system, and all seemed well for a moment.

But I wasn't aware that one gunner had decided to fill his walk-around bottle with oxygen just in case we experienced more trouble. As flight engineer, I wouldn't have allowed it for two reasons: it wasn't really necessary, and at 60 degrees below zero the valve can freeze open. The gunner finished filling his portable bottle, and shortly after disconnecting from the oxygen system, he heard the squeal of a leak and yelled for help. The valve had not been able to completely close.

Ever hear the saying, "When in trouble, when in doubt, run in circles, scream and shout?" That statement would have captured the feeling of our dilemma exactly. Of course, I didn't really think of it then, let alone say it. Circumstances were far too serious for that kind of nonsense. All attempts to stop the leak failed and we lost the second oxygen system.

The B-17 had three oxygen systems. With only one system still operating every man had to share his mask or tube with another crewman. We still had a great distance left on our return flight. We were flying at 29,500 feet while enemy fighters looked for crippled or lagging planes.

Our pilot, Bill, called me out of the turret to inform me of his plan. He said, "We only have enough oxygen left for two crewmen, and we must remain in formation. There is little fighter opposition at the moment, so I'm going to give the order to bail out. I want you to stay in your turret and we can take this ship home."

Bill choked up as he ordered, "Bail Out!" Everyone took it real hard.

One crewman shouted, "I'm a Jew! I don't want to be taken prisoner!"

Several others called out, saying that we could fight our way home down on the deck, flying at 20 - 50 feet above ground. Fighters hate to attempt an attack there.

The difficulty would be in getting from here to the ground. We were flying above thick clouds that concealed the mountains below – not the ideal place to descend. Bill replied, "If everybody wants to try it, we will."

Each man agreed to stay with the ship. So instead of having the men bail out, Bill slid the B-17 out of formation and put it in a steep glide. We went through the clouds only to find another layer below. Praying that we would find a valley, we kept going down and soon saw a mountain on our right. There were still more clouds, but we used that mountain as a guide as if climbing down its side.

Soon, we could see the ground just below us. Ground without ice! We knew our ship had reached the deck. Then I learned that one of our waist gunners had passed out from lack of oxygen. The other waist gunner kept working with him until he regained consciousness.

It was peaceful now. The area was flat with no artillery shells or enemy fighters. Flying over farms, we saw far ahead of us a large two-wheeled cart drawn by a single horse. A girl was pitching hay into the wagon. She took off her bonnet and waved a friendly hello as we roared past like a pelican flying just above the bay. We came within about one hundred yards of her, and her horse just about bolted. What a blessing it was to see such warmth from a stranger after the terrifying ordeal we had been through. The weary men were suddenly refreshed by the sight and nearly climbed out of the plane as her golden locks fell out from under her bonnet. I wondered . . . was she really being friendly, or was she thinking that a gunner from this monstrous plane might shoot her? I doubt that any of the men ever forgot the encounter.

With a brave pilot and a devoted crew, we arrived safely back at Great Ashfield and every crewman walked off the plane. You probably guessed it – Captain Clark was welcomed back with a chewing-out for falling out of formation and taking the chance through the mountains. But our pilot had broad shoulders, and he had made tough choices before. He took it all in stride, knowing all his men were back on home base.

The Sovereign Lord is my strength!
He will make me as surefooted as a deer
and bring me safely over the mountains.
Habakkuk 3:19 NLT

Tour of Duty Completed

Frederichshafen, Germany, was the first mission after returning to duty. It was a very long haul. This was really hard on us after having ten days of rest. Two days later we went to Brunswick, always a very hard target, but we met little opposition except flak. The next day we went to Ostend-Middelkerke. It turned out to be an easy trip.

It was my last mission. I had actually completed a tour of combat duty. The odds for a crewman completing a tour seemed hopeless, so it was a grand day of celebration when someone did finish. What a surprise to see a group waiting at the hardstand to greet me when our plane had landed. Some of these men I had never even met before. Some were hometown friends that I had known for a long time.

Among those I knew were Group Personnel, Sergeant Major Everett Beavers, 385th Red Cross Field Director, Boussey Butler, Base Hospital physician, Captain Patilla, and Armament NCO, Master Sergeant Bradford Myers. I didn't know Bradford Myers before coming to England. Later I learned that he was from Anson and we developed a friendship during my time at Great Ashfield. Butler and Beavers had been school teachers in my home town and Captain Patilla was the family physician for the community in and around Anson, Texas.

They were congratulating me, patting me on the back, and asking if they could talk with me about my missions. One gentleman insisted I take a ride on his Harley. I tried to explain to him that I had never ridden a motorcycle of any kind, let alone a Harley. He wouldn't take no for an answer. He said that after all I'd done that I couldn't go home without experiencing the thrill. So I followed his instruction and actually rode the length of the airstrip and back again. Any other time I would have been shot for a stunt like that. The young man was right – it was quite a thrill.

Ex-Teacher, 2 Students Are Together in England

BY FLEM HALL,
(Star Telegram's own correspondent in European theater).

ENGLAND.—A teacher and two former students of Anson High School are serving on the same 8th AAF Liberator base, 5,000 miles from the West Texas city where they last saw one another.

The former teacher is James E. Beaver, sergeant major of the personnel section where members of both flying and ground crews are classified.

The ex-students are Lt. James C. Hestand, a radio communications officer, and Tech. Sgt. Bradford L. Myers, a chief armorer in charge of loading bombs into the big ships and keeping their machineguns in slick working order.

"I suppose it's the answer to every schoolboy's prayer," says Lieutenant Hestand, "to find himself an officer and his former teacher an enlisted man, but in reality it doesn't mean a thing. I respect Sergeant Beaver just as I did in school. The lessons he taught me have served me well."

After serving at Anson, Beaver, now 34, went to Caddo where he was superintendent of schools when he entered the armed services. He is the son of Mr. and Mrs. Baxter Beaver of Anson. He holds both B. A. and master's degrees from the University of Texas.

Lieutenant Hestand, 23, is the son of Mr. and Mrs. Robert M. Hestand, Anson. He worked for Montgomery Ward at Abilene before enlisting two years ago.

Sergeant Myers is the son of Mr. and Mrs. William B. Myers, former neighbors of the Hestand's.

THE STARS AND STRIPES
Daily Newspaper for U.S. Armed Forces – European Theater of Operations New York, N.Y. – London, England

Five thousand miles from where it was started in Anson some years ago a Spanish lesson is resumed at an 8th Air Force Base in England. Sgt. James Beaver, center, is the former teacher; Tech. Sgt. Bradford Myers, left, and Lt. James Hestand are the former students of the high school class.

Most of my crew needed one more mission – some needed several.

I was offered a battlefield commission to second lieutenant, but I turned it down. Right then, the Army Air Corp didn't seem to be the career I wanted, especially if it meant taking a desk job or an instructing position. I would live to regret it, but at that time I was disillusioned with some of the generals in command.

I specifically disagreed with the strategy of one commander, General Doolittle. I realize the history books shine on him, and a lot of experts consider him a military mastermind. But it was his orders to fly for seven days without a break that almost wiped out the Eighth Air Force. This not only put the men in a weakened state, but also put our ground crews at a disadvantage trying to keep the planes readied for flight.

The success of our missions had been averaging a 95 percent destruction rate on enemy targets. Doolittle's scheme took us from 95 percent down to five percent! He did in seven days what the Luftwaffe had never been able to do. I heard a rumor that someone from Washington halted the strategy.

On the other hand, General Curtis E. LeMay, Colonel Vandevanter, and Major Tesla were great men who lived up to their reputation. I admired them and held them in the highest esteem.

Your unfailing love, oh Lord, is as vast as the heavens;
your faithfulness reaches beyond the clouds.
Psalm 36:5 NLT

Fort Hero Vandevanter Named Full Colonel at 26

AN EIGHTH BOMBER STATION, Jan. 7—Twenty-six-year-old Elliott Vandevanter Jr., of Washington, the youngest commander of a heavy-bomb group in the ETO and one of the youngest in any theater, today was promoted to a full colonel.

Col. Vandevanter, West Pointer and Fortress pilot with the 19th Bomb Group, which operated in the Pacific in the early days of the war, has led his B17 group and combat wing on numerous missions over Germany and Occupied Europe.

His decorations include the Silver Star, DFC, Air Medal and Cluster.

THE STARS AND STRIPES
Daily Newspaper for U.S. Armed Forces – European Theater of Operations New York, N.Y. – London, England

HEADQUARTERS
385TH BOMBARDMENT GROUP (H)
U. S. ARMY AIR FORCES
APO 559

C-B-26

27 April 1944.

SUBJECT: COMPLETION OF OPERATIONAL TOUR OF COMBAT DUTY.

TO   : WHOM IT MAY CONCERN.

1. Technical Sergeant Oral F. Lindsey, 38230452, 550th Bombardment Squadron, 385th Bombardment Group (H), has this date completed an operational tour of combat duty in heavy bombardment aircraft over enemy occupied Continental Europe.

2. He has flown as a Top Turret Gunner on a B-17 "Flying Fortress" in the bombing of many important enemy objectives. Some of the more important ones were the following: Ludwigshafen, Germany on the 7th of January 1944; Frankfurt, Germany on the 8th of February 1944; Berlin, Germany on the 8th of March 1944; and Politz, Germany on the 11th of April 1944. While participating in a heavy bombardment mission over Tutow, Germany, his formation was attacked by enemy fighter planes and in the air battle that ensued, he succeeded in sending one (1) enemy plane plunging to the earth in flames. On numerous other occasions, T/Sgt. Lindsey warded off the enemy planes by his accurate fire and enabled his plane to return to its base safely. His performance of duty has been "excellent."

3. The following awards have been presented to Technical Sergeant Oral F. Lindsey:

AIR MEDAL
1st Oak Leaf Cluster
2nd Oak Leaf Cluster
3rd Oak Leaf Cluster
DISTINGUISHED FLYING CROSS

4. In view of his past experience as a combat gunner and his ability to perform his duties in an excellent manner, and since it is his desire to remain with the Group as a Gunnery Instructor, it is hereby recommended that he be retained in the Group as such.

E. VANDEVANTER, JR.,
Colonel, Air Corps,
Commanding.

124

AM for five missions   R E S T R I C T E D   (G-B-O)

GENERAL ORDERS)   Hq 3d Bombardment Division
:   APO 634
No.   31)   E X T R A C T   2 February   1944

Under the provisions of Army Regulations 600-45, 8 August 1932, as amended, and pursuant to authority contained in Section I, Circular 36, Hq ETOUSA, 5 April 1943, and teletype 3163ZC Hq VIII Bomber Command, 26 September 1943, the AIR MEDAL is awarded to the following-named EM.

Citation: For exceptionally meritorious achievement, while participating in five separate bomber combat missions over enemy occupied Continental ████████████████ ██████████████ ███ill displayed by this EM upon these occasions reflects great credit upon himself and the Armed Forces of the United States.

ORAL F. LINDSEY,   , Staff Sergeant, 550th Bombardment Squadron (H), Army Air Forces, United States Army. Home Address: Rt #2, Stamford, Texas.

By command of Brigadier General LE MAY: A. W. KISSNER
Colonel, Air Corps GSC
OFFICIAL: Chief of Staff

O. T. DASWELL
Major, Air Corps
Adjutant General   R E S T R I C T E D

D. F. C.   R E S T R I C T E D   (G-A-10)

GENERAL ORDERS)   Hq Eighth Air Force
:   APO 634
NO.   224)   E X T R A C T   29 March   1944

Under the provisions of Army Regulations 600-45, 22 September 1943, and pursuant to authority contained in Restricted TT Message #2159, Hq ████████, 11 January 1944, the DISTINGUISHED FLYING CROSS is awarded to the following-named e/m for extraordinary achievement, as set forth in citation. This individual has previously earned the Air Medal and three Oak Leaf Clusters for wear therewith:

ORAL F. LINDSEY, 38230432, Technical Sergeant, 550th Bombardment Squadron (M), Army Air Forces, United States Army. For extraordinary achievement while serving as Top Turret Gunner of a B-17 airplane on twenty heavy bombardment missions over enemy occupied Continental Europe. Displaying great courage and skill, Sergeant Lindsey, fighting from his gun position, has destroyed one enemy airplane and has materially aided in the success of each of the twenty missions. The courage, coolness, and skill displayed by Sergeant Lindsey on all these occasions reflect the highest credit upon himself and the Armed Forces of the United States. Home Address: Stamford, Texas.

By command of Lieutenant General DOOLITTLE:

OFFICIAL: JOHN A. SAMFORD
Brigadier General, U.S.A.
EDWARD E. TORO   Chief of Staff
Colonel, AGD
Adjutant General

                  R E S T R I C T E D

OLC for destruction of E/A R E S T R I C T E D   G-A-O

GENERAL ORDERS)   Hq Eighth Air Force
                :   APO 634
NO.   164)   E X T R A C T   14 March   1944

    Under the provisions of Army Regulations 600-45, 22 September 1943, and
pursuant to authority contained in Restricted TT Message #2139, Hq USSAFE, 11
January 1944, an OAK LEAF CLUSTER is awarded to the following-named__ EM ___,
in addition to the Air Medal previously awarded.
    Citation: For meritorious achievement in the destruction of one enemy air-
plane, while serving as crewman on a bombardment mission over enemy occupied
Continental Europe. The courage, coolness and skill displayed by this EM
upon this occasion reflect great credit upon himself and the Armed Forces of the
United States.
*   *   *
ORAL F. LINDSEY,   , Technical Sergeant, 550th Bombardment Squadron (H),
Army Air Forces, United States Army. Home Address: Stamford, Texas. (Third OLC)

*   *   *
           By command of Major General DOOLITTLE:

OFFICIAL:

EDWARD E. TORO
Colonel, AGD
Actg Adjutant General   R E S T R I C T E D   78*

Honoring the Yanks!

When a soldier had completed a tour of combat, he would usually be sent back to the US if he wanted to go home. Most of us did, and I was one of them. We went to London to the Eighth Air Force Headquarters to get our orders. Headquarters was set up in a huge hotel. Some of it was used as sleeping quarters for military personnel, including those like me that were being processed out. Those of us that were just passing through would take-up temporary quarters in the hotel in one of the bays that was filled with bunks. It served as a sort of a holding tank. We wouldn't be assigned any duties or responsibilities; we would just hang around until time for departure.

A young man who was showing me through the place pointed to a guy on one of the bunks and said, "That's Mickey Rooney!" I know he'd love to meet you. He really likes talking with the men who have finished their missions."

He was out cold. I said, "Man, don't wake him up." It would have been exciting to meet him, but to disturb him would have been cruel, I thought. So I went on to the office and got my orders.

As I walked back to my quarters, I began to feel like I was walking through a dream. So many men I knew hadn't survived the war. Even when I first began my missions, I had never dared to believe that I would make it home. Now all that was left for me to do was sit and wait for a ship that would take me back to the States.

One day I was just lying in the sack when an officer stepped into the bay. He ordered me to fall out in a class A uniform and to be sure to wear all medals. As usual with the military, there was no explanation, just the command.

The British officials had asked our officers to assist in conducting a parade of the combat crews, so the English would have the opportunity to see them and to show their appreciation. They managed to get 400 men assembled at Leicester Square.

The British general made a speech to the English home folks. He said, "These are the remaining few that have done that which was believed to be impossible – flying missions to Germany in daylight. The crews of the B-17 and B-24 Heavy Bombers bore a heavier percentage of losses than any other outfit and they are the most decorated. These brave men defeated the Luftwaffe when their leaders chose to use large formations and learned to strategically stack the airplanes for the most effective defense."

Our colonel took the microphone and related the story of General Eaker's response to the USAAF generals who said that daylight bombing was impossible. General Eaker had said, in effect – just watch!

The colonel also complimented the British general and thanked him for his generous praise of the USAAF. He explained that the general was being modest by not mentioning the fact that the RAF pilots were highly skilled and had always been out-numbered by the enemy but still completed many successful missions. The colonel went on to say, "We could never have succeeded in saturation bombing as the British Royal Air Force did, for example, on Hamburg, Germany. In addition, the crews of the RAF took out every dam in Germany on those night missions. This made it possible for our men to concentrate on accurate pinpoint bombing on targets that were difficult to find even in the daylight. And for that daylight, we paid a price.

There was a time early on when completing five missions was considered to be the average, and indeed about only one crew in twenty completed fifteen missions."

After the speeches were made, we began the parade that probably extended for two miles through Leicester Square and on to Piccadilly Circus. The USAAF band was led by the color guard. We followed, marching in "locked step" or formation fashion. This was a mixed group of men from different squadrons. Many of the men had earned Purple Hearts, and some limped as they kept in step. Otherwise, all were in good form.

On-lookers waved small flags, US and British flags alike; whatever they could get their hands on. Our soldiers threw coins to the children until they had no coins left. Then a few men started throwing out pound notes, each of which was equivalent to four American dollars. The children had already been excited over getting a sixpence or shilling before our men graduated to tossing out florin and half-crowns. Of course they went wild over the pound notes! Our officers soon put a stop to this, knowing that the children would be in danger if things got out of control. With only 400 men and perhaps as many as 100,000 children spread over the two-mile parade, I'm afraid that most left disappointed.

It was the most thrilling parade of my life and one of the most rewarding events I have ever experienced. I felt honored to have been included in such company.

The one who plants and the one who waters
work as a team with the same purpose. Yet they will be rewarded
individually, according to their own... work.
I Corinthians 3:8 NLT

Return to the States

Fire on the RMS Mauretania II

We were going home and it seemed everyone was celebrating. This was a Cunard White Star liner, specifically the RMS Mauretania II. We weren't crowded like we had been on the Queen Elizabeth (another White Star ship) coming over to England. The ship had been put into military service but still carried civilians. The military personnel were all assigned to either guard duty (submarine watch) or KP. I chose guard duty. The voyage to the States would take five or six days, but trouble would start almost immediately. I had just thought that all the excitement was behind me.

I was just killing time when I heard someone call for help and ran to see what was going on. I saw an old friend of mine, Sergeant Liner. We had met back in Wendover, Utah, while we were in gunnery school. Liner was in a corner armed with only an MP club and fighting about a dozen men. I saw his armband and realized he was officially on guard duty. I would have taken his side anyway. It appeared that a bunch of drunks had gotten out of control, but between the two of us we made short work of them.

When bodies quit flying and the punches stopped, I asked Liner, "What's this all about, anyway?"

Liner was exhausted and was trying to catch his breath. He said, "It was an argument between the soldiers and this British cadet. They had the kid down on the deck and wouldn't break it up. You can see I'm on guard duty. I could have summoned backup, but I didn't blow the whistle 'cause I hated to get some of these guys thrown in the brig or get busted."

Hearing this, I checked with the cadet; he didn't want to make anything of it. It seemed he started the brawl by saying that America should still belong to Britain.

I said to him, "Are you crazy? You had better not say that when you are in the States!"

Liner sent him away with a warning to keep his opinions to himself if he didn't want to get killed.

I had to ask, "Liner, are you always in trouble or just when I come along? This makes the third time! There was the incident where the two perverts were assaulting two other soldiers much smaller than them. And you can't forget the time at Wendover when those guys set fire to the cedars and dang near killed us!"

While we were reminiscing, trouble was brewing again. We heard another ruckus, and sure enough the little Brit was in the thick of it. He wasn't very smart, but he sure had a lot of spunk. The cadet was persistent about his cause, and the men jumped him again.

By the time we got to him, they had him draped over the railing ready to throw him overboard. The two of us were barely able to drag his boney carcass back onto the deck. He was bloody and had both eyes blacked. Liner asked him if he was suicidal and he proudly exclaimed, "Well, I'm right about America!"

I said, "You're being ridiculous and you're gonna get yourself killed!"

Liner explained to the cadet that next time we may not be able to stop them. He said, "I'm ordering you to stay in your quarters – for your own sake!"

He finally promised Liner that he would, and we didn't have any more trouble. I don't know if he actually spent the rest of the voyage in his quarters, but at least he stayed out of sight.

In the meantime our guys were really bent out of shape. They looked at me and said, "You're not even a guard."

I told him, "That's not required, and I'm not going to stand by and watch a gang take out my buddy."

Liner said, "Look, we're on your side. I'm trying to keep you guys out of the brig. And if you had killed that kid you'd be settin' up residence in Leavenworth! You're goin' home to your families. Now break it up!"

Afterwards we were assessing damages, and it seemed Liner's guardian angels were still working overtime – I couldn't believe he wasn't even bleeding!

He complained, "Yeah, but I'm sure gonna be sore for a spell. I'm bruised all over!"

While he covered his watch we visited for a while and tried to catch up on the latest news. Later, when Liner's shift was over, I retired to my bunk for some shut-eye. We saw very little of each other the rest of the trip and only briefly after we landed in the States. I have never been able to make contact with him since the war.

By the next day we were well out to sea and had hit a storm. Although it was somewhat small, it was bad enough to make some men sick. But that was nothing. About mid-ocean, a real storm hit us. Water nearly waist deep was coming across the deck, driving everyone below.

I was on submarine watch and remained on deck as long as possible, but my skinny body and a uniform wasn't enough against the sweeping blow of sea water. Finally, I was forced to retreat below.

Soon after I had surrendered to the storm, the fire signal blared, and it was no drill. A cigarette had been tossed into a litter can, and there was no one in that area when it caught fire, so the whole area was engulfed before anyone noticed. It was only the paint on the walls burning, they said, but it was as impressive as a two-story house fully engulfed in flames.

The English sailors were magnificent. With the storm rolling the ship hard, sea water making the deck slick, and the fire already out of control, they went right into it with their hoses. They were driven back three times by the extreme heat and slick deck, but they finally cooled it down enough that they went in and finished it off.

While this went on, a British officer (not a fire marshal) talked to me. He said, "The ship is in no danger of sinking and the fire will not be spreading. These men know their work and the Mauretania has fire-proof bulkheads that will not allow the fire to spread."

I was sure glad to hear this. I'm more afraid of fire than I ever was of bullets. If we had been in trouble, the nearest help was 800 miles away, and with such a storm, rescue would have been almost impossible. These firemen knew that and knew they were the only hope. I had the utmost respect and gratitude for these fearless men.

After the fire was out, the raging storm continued. Those of us that had guard duty continued our assigned rotating shifts on deck. There weren't supposed to be any German subs left, but we couldn't take the chance that it might not be true. It was difficult standing on deck with the wind and ocean swells slapping over the rails of the Mauretania. By the end of a shift I was completely exhausted. We were greatly relieved when the storm finally subsided. It had lasted for the better part of two days.

The Lord says, "I will rescue those who love me.
I will protect those who trust in my name.
When they call on me, I will answer;
I will be with them in trouble.
I will rescue them and honor them."
Psalm 91:14-15 NLT

Galveston Island to Ardmore, Oklahoma

After finishing my missions, I was sent back to the States and given thirty days leave. It was kind of like coming back from the dead. It was good to be home, but it was also sad because I knew that nearly all our old bunch was in a prison camp or dead.

I ended up at Galveston instructing flight engineers and teaching them "air to air" and "air to ground" gunnery. This was about as exciting as a knitting party to me.

Luckily for me, I met a major who was forming a new outfit to go to combat. He said he didn't have a flight engineer and I told him I would like to have that position on his crew. He was a little skeptical that I'd really do it, but we agreed to fly the next day.

I said, "If you're not comfortable flying with me, then tell me. And if I have any doubts about being on your crew, I'll admit it."

The next morning, Major Charlie Glenn came out to the airplane and found me sitting on the hardstand. I got up, saluted him and said, "It's ready to go."

In the air when we had leveled out, the major started to trim the ailerons and elevator. He looked at me and said, "Did you do something to this airplane?"

I said, "Yes, I loaded it with the slip-stick to 32 degrees M.A.C."

He was real impressed and said, "They didn't do that for us in training."

When we landed he said, "I've made my mind up, how about you?"

I said, "I did that yesterday. I want to go back."

He was satisfied with me but said, "I don't think you know what you're in for." He explained that first we would have to get a squadron together, match up crews, and go through flight training.

I said, "Major, I've already had experience with all that. I can't possibly do it alone, but I'm a pretty good judge of character and can delegate some of the real work to others."

At this particular base on Galveston Island we were training men that would ultimately become replacements for crews overseas. Major Glenn would be looking for seven good flight engineers as there were seven planes to each *new* squadron. Altogether, four squadrons were being prepared for combat. Overseas a squadron consisted of 14 crews but a commanding officer would only bring in seven new crews and match them with seven experienced crews to create a refreshed squadron.

I found the new flight engineers very well-trained, and all the other lead men reported the same. After making our selections and assigning the men to crews, we were ready for final testing as teams. The men we had trained and selected for our squadron took first place in the competition over the other three squadrons.

From Galveston Island we were sent to Ardmore Army Airfield (known to many of us as Gene Autry Field) in Oklahoma. At this facility the crewmen would participate in more advanced training involving gunnery, navigation, and flying formation. They would even have the chance to practice flying formation. When the men finished this step they would be taking a long train ride to Seattle, Washington.

I wrote my folks frequently from Ardmore about my duties there, but didn't explain that it was preparing me for another tour of duty overseas. Through experience I had learned that you couldn't always depend on things turning out the way you planned. I saw no reason to concern my parents, especially my mom.

While I was stationed at Ardmore AAF my brother, Arvin, drove his 1929 Model-A Ford to Ardmore. He was bringing my parents, along with his wife, Nell, and their daughter, Wanda, for a surprise visit. I would have been waiting to greet them if I had known ahead of time.

Visit From Family
Oral with his mother, Elmina Ridgeway Lindsey, during the family's visit to Ardmore AAF, Ardmore, Oklahoma

The first person they met at the squadron was Major Glenn. As soon as he received word that I had visitors, he hopped into his vehicle and met up with them. He instructed the ground crew to ready the airplane for a demonstration. By the time I reached the hangar, everyone was already out at the airplane.

My mother said that Major Glenn was the nicest person she ever met. She told me he had claimed that I had been a great help to him and the squadron and said, "He's done a lot to get this outfit ready for combat."

My mother asked him, "Surely he's not going with you?"

The major asked, "You mean to tell me that you didn't know?"

I quickly changed the subject by directing their attention to the airplane. My dad was not impressed with the plane's armor plating. He said, "What is this supposed to stop?"

I said, "It won't stop bullets, but it stops a lot of shrapnel from flak shells."

My dad was more impressed with the Sperry Top Turret with its computing sight. He was also amazed that the unit was completely equipped with all the electrical stuff as well as having the guns, ammo, and oxygen. Dad was especially intrigued when he noticed that none of the equipment or wiring was disturbed by the turret turning around and around.

I proceeded to show him how to operate it, then told him when you close that dead-man switch these little amplidyne motors will go from stop to 38,000 rpm in about two seconds. Then you can steer anywhere you want and you can't shoot your own wing, propellers, or tail. You have an automatic cut-off switch that prevents that.

My mother also tried out the turret, but when the amplidyne motors screamed, she quit. I told her that I listened to them for hours on every mission. That's nothing – you should hear my .50 calibers when they start hammering! The whole airplane shakes when thirteen of these fifties open up. It only takes a few minutes for them to eat up the 8,000 rounds we carried.

Boeing Flying Fortress B-17s Line Up
USAF photo courtesy of National Archives at College Park, MD
Photo Research and Reproduction
by Robert McMahan Photography
(Photo not taken at Ardmore, Oklahoma)

The family was really impressed with the courteous treatment that everyone gave them. My mother said that they were treated like royalty; it was much different than the things she had heard about the military. I explained to them that this was not at all like the training camps when you first enlist.

When my family had left the base Major Glenn really chewed me out for not letting my folks know about my upcoming mission.

I said, "I figured there was no use in them worrying about something that might not happen anyway."

After this brief break in my duties I proceeded to complete the tasks at hand. Soon we would be ready for the long train ride to Seattle, Washington, to prepare the new Boeing B-17 that was to be issued to us. Everyone was excited knowing that we were another step closer to the orders that would most likely be sending us overseas.

The master was full of praise. 'Well done,
my good and faithful servant.
You have been faithful in handling this small amount,
so now I will give you many more responsibilities.
Let's celebrate together!'
Matthew 25:21 NLT

Trouble on the Train

The day finally came that we would begin our trip to Seattle, Washington, to pick up our new B-17's. We would be based at Moses Lake while we prepared for our trip to England. Actually, none of us knew where we would be stationed, but we were fairly sure it would be England.

Major Glenn called me and said he wanted me to be in charge of the troop train. He said, "I know there will be master sergeants on board, but not one of them could control these men if they start drinking. This is a rough bunch and it's going to be a long trip."

I accepted the task and said, "I'll need some men to help carry foot lockers, supplies, and records. Also, I want one man as a partner or bodyguard."

Major Glenn said, "You're going to be the one responsible. Do it your way."

I thought of at least a dozen capable men that wouldn't be afraid if trouble started. But there was an Oklahoma boy that transferred over from the infantry. He had a foot crippled when he caught two machine-gun bullets while serving in Italy. I knew this guy wouldn't panic and do something wrong if it came down to a fight.

He laughed when I asked him to be my backup and said, "Sure, it'll be a piece of cake. I've done this before, and you can bet there will be trouble."

This would be a three-day trip on a train carrying around 500 soldiers, including administrative personnel, cooks, bakers, gunners, and everyone it takes to make a squadron. Some had combat experience but most were going overseas for their first tour. They would be settling into boredom soon with nothing to do but look out the window.

We loaded up and boarded the train. The first thing I did was to get everyone's attention.

I said, "I'm going to be in charge of the troop train. All of you here know me. We want to have a great time, and hopefully, see a lot of the country. There will be no gambling and no whiskey. I can't be everywhere at once and I'm not out to catch anyone. As long as there's no trouble, we'll keep it that way. But if there is trouble, you'd better believe me when I say that the troublemakers will be taken care of." I knew there would be a lot of whiskey on board, and there's always one that's just got to show everyone how tough he is.

Just a few hours after we pulled out of the station in Oklahoma, a young man ran up to me and said, "Come quick! I think a sergeant is going to shoot somebody!"

I told him to stay behind us and we went to the indicated car. Two master sergeants were brandishing their Colt .45's and talking loudly. They were frightening the civilians riding in the car with them. I kept my cap pulled down to hide my face and casually walked up to the one standing in the aisle with his gun in the air.

Then I was on him like paint on a red barn. I was sure the pistol would be loaded and could see the safety was off. I jammed the web of my hand in front of the Colt's hammer just as he pulled the trigger! The gun did not fire because the hammer hit the web of my hand just as I had planned. The government issue Colt .45 is a single-action pistol, so there was no concern if the sergeant pulled the trigger again. The gun was unable to fire until the slide was actuated or the hammer manually cocked. Having control of the sergeant's weapon now I twisted it from his hand as hard as I could. It would have served him right if his finger had gotten broken in the process. He lost some hide and a little blood, but his trigger finger was in one piece.

My partner had his .45 pointed in the face of the other master sergeant, who immediately laid his gun on the seat. He wasn't the instigator here and wanted no more trouble. I saw Okie take the gun and unload it. We sat these men down, took their whiskey, and threatened them with a court-martial.

I apologized to the older couple that they had been showing off to. The lady said, "He was bragging and I was very afraid of him."

I assured her, "Well, they won't bother you anymore. In fact, we'll be collecting the guns from every soldier and taking their whiskey."

At this, one young soldier stood up and said, "Well, you won't take my whiskey!"

Before he could even complete the sentence, I grabbed his bottle and shoved him back in his seat saying, "You wanna watch me pour it out?"

He actually followed us to the back of the car and watched me pour the whiskey down the wash basin. I thought he was going to cry. I went back and said, "Anybody else want to contribute to the basin? It's not stopped up."

My buddy and I went through the cars and took up all the guns. Luckily, we had lockers to store them in until we reached Seattle. The men would be able to get their weapons at the end of the line. The guns were easily identified by their serial number. The soldiers were required to carry a card identifying their weapon and most men had theirs memorized.

Okie and I also gathered any whiskey bottles that were out in the open. Most of the men were smart enough to hide their bottles.

The next day the master sergeant was sober, and he was sore in more ways than one. He complained about his ribs hurting, his torn finger, and the whiskey that I poured out. He said, "I'd give anything if you'd take off that gun and badge and meet me in Seattle."

He was really a big man, six-foot tall and weighed about two-hundred pounds. I paused and asked him if he knew of a particular street in Seattle. He said that he did, so I said, "The cops don't go there, and nobody would notice a fight." It was agreed then, and we never spoke again during the trip.

We had little trouble with people drinking after that episode, and the soldiers playing cards kept their money hidden. I didn't bother anyone that wasn't making trouble.

We must have stopped a hundred times. Sometimes there would be time for the troops to get off, stretch their legs, and take a break. Finally, we pulled into Seattle and unloaded. The records and guns were handed over to the officers there, and they took charge of them. As I put my .45 in the locker, I saw the eager master sergeant waiting for me. So I took off my armband and badge and threw them in the locker, too. Without a word we headed for a street in town just a few blocks away.

I said, "We agreed to one on one. So why is your friend coming along?"

The master sergeant said, "Oh, he's just going to see that it's a fair fight."

Just then I could hear someone coming up behind me. I looked back and saw my old buddy coming toward us dragging that bad leg. I turned and said to the sergeant, "OK then, we'll keep it fair."

He raised his voice and said, "I'm not going if this guy goes along!"

I said, "In other words I fight both of you or there's no fight." He didn't dispute me or even make a comment.

We made fun of them and went on back to our bunch at the train station. Soon the buses arrived to take us to our barracks.

It is safer to meet a bear robbed of her cubs
than to confront a fool caught in folly.
Proverbs 17:12 NLT

Under the Silver Lining (A Real Lemon)

The new B-17's were impressive, and we were excited looking forward to our new airplanes. We learned that squadron commanders would get plush cockpits. The other airplanes we had flown in didn't have upholstery at all, just bare sheet metal.

I warned the new flight engineers that new airplanes always came with a few bugs and would need adjustments before they would be dependable. With this in mind I went to our new plane and noticed immediately that the trim tabs were upside down. Inside I saw a very nice looking, new smelling airplane, but I heard a buzzing sound that I didn't recognize. After further investigation I discovered an oxygen leak – a very dangerous thing. Next, I saw a lot of hydraulic fluid and then located that leak. Under the co-pilot's seat was supposed to be a small generator that provided vacuum for the pilot's gyro. It was missing. In just a brief check of this new plane I had observed three things that would ground an airplane even for a local flight.

We hadn't seen anything yet. There were so many write-ups that I told the crew chief I would reject the airplane and my pilot would back me up. He called the engineering officer, who came out fighting mad.

I said, "Captain, if you believe in this piece of junk then come and make the test flight with us."

Now he was really hot. He said, "Gladly! My crew chief will fix all of this in time to fly it tomorrow."

Tomorrow came with more bad news. The crew chief told his captain, "Some of the parts needed to repair the plane were not available. That's not all. We probably haven't even found half of the problems."

The captain was in a rage and wanted to call in a colonel. Major Glenn said, "We'll still take it up for a test flight if you go along."

Sentimental Journey – Restored B-17G of CAF, Arizona Wing
(New planes were no longer being painted.)
Britt Dietz Photographer – Photo Used with Permission

With a skeleton crew we took off and climbed to 10,000 feet. At that elevation we could run all our checks, such as feathering a propeller. Major Glenn was piloting the plane and the engineering officer was in the co-pilot seat.

The major said, "Now let's check the autopilot."

The autopilot was set up and turned on, and it instantly tried to put the airplane into a roll. Major Glenn had the controls and saved us from a disaster. The autopilot was set again and turned on. This time the major and the captain both held the controls. Again, it tried to roll the plane. The autopilot was written off as a total loss.

The engineering officer had calmed down some now, but he said, "You will take the aircraft as is or you will be grounded."

The major was a much better pilot than the captain. In so many words Major Glenn let the officer know that and added, "We'll take this piece of junk off your hands, but you will sign off on every 'red cross' on this form. If anything goes wrong, the whole mess will end up in your lap!"

I cry out to the Lord; I plead for the Lord's mercy.
I pour out my complaints before him and tell him all my troubles.
I look for someone to come and help me,
but no one gives me a passing thought!
No one will help me; no one cares a bit what happens to me.
Psalm 142:1, 2,4   NLT

Mission Adventures
Second Tour

Snowed-In at Reykjavik

The days we spent at Boeing were hectic. Time that should have been spent coordinating our plans for the long trip ahead was spent on the faulty airplane. Finally, the airplane checked out well enough that we were ready to go.

The flight was uneventful and without concern until we were to land at Goose Bay, Labrador. Major Glenn was from Florida and had never landed on ice. I assured him it would be easy. We would pour strong bleach (STB – Super-Tropical-Bleach) on the tires so they would not slip. Also, the cold was on our side. It would be below zero, and ice isn't slick at low temperatures.

The snow was ten to twelve feet deep on the level – absolutely a beautiful sight. The ground crew at Goose Bay had just been clearing the runway for our arrival. These massive snowplows bulldozed through the snow forcing it to the sides and created a canyon with snow banks up to twenty feet deep. Major Glenn made a perfect landing with no slipping or sliding. Our only challenge now was climbing out of this frozen canyon. Once we made it over the snow bank some of the men rode in snow-crawling vehicles while the rest of us walked to our barracks. Here we entered the second floor because the ground floor was completely buried in the deep snow.

I had seen plenty of snow before, but never anything like this. It was an exciting experience, but we were all glad to leave there for a more moderate climate. We flew past Greenland and headed for Meeks Field near Reykjavik, Iceland. The weather forecast predicted stormy conditions around our destination. The flight from

Goose Bay to Meeks Field would be a long haul, but we were well prepared with full fuel tanks and the advantage of a light load.

The new airplane was still performing okay, but since we had no autopilot the officers took turns flying it manually. A B-17 had no power assist such as power steering on a car. With no autopilot it took all the muscle you had to move the rudder, elevators, or ailerons. After several hours a pilot would be completely exhausted.

Along with the other aircraft from Seattle, we landed safely in Reykjavik. Weather conditions weren't too bad when we arrived. There was only light snow and some sleet forming as the storm front made its way to Iceland. The weather soon changed to rain with wind gusts to 30 mph. When the front came through, the temperature dropped to zero with winds increasing to 70 mph, and everything was covered with a sheet of ice and snow. By morning snowdrifts were ten feet deep and the temperature was holding steady at zero. The wind, however, had dropped to only 40 mph.

The storm's high winds brought so much ice and snow that the runway conditions were too dangerous for a plane to make a takeoff. It was official – we would remain grounded for the duration of the storm.

Later that day I went to the Red Cross and met a girl named Cele Helbock. I was told she was the only woman on base. She was very friendly, and pretty, too. I spent as much time as possible with her during the eleven days we were snowed in. Before our crew had to leave, she promised she would never forget me, and I made her the same promise. Of course, I knew that working at the Red Cross she met hundreds of men. But I was young, and when someone made me a promise, I looked at their eyes to discern the truth. I was seldom wrong in my judgment about a man or a woman. I believed Cele was sincere.

Finally, the storm passed, making it possible for the runway to be cleared of snow. We loaded up and took off for England.

What's more, I will be with you,
and I will protect you wherever you go.
I will someday bring you safely back to this land.
I will be with you constantly
until I have finished giving you everything I have promised.
Genesis 28:15 NLT

Irresistible Force Meets Immovable Object

We arrived at Debach Station, an airfield northwest of Woodbridge, England to join up with the 493rd Bomb Group of the 863rd Squadron. The grueling trip was over and we were all anxious to get down to business. But our relief was short-lived.

We were informed that all of our crews were being split up. Everything Major Glenn had strategically put together was destroyed with one simple command. The major was a man of integrity who earned the respect and trust of his men. I had been looking forward to serving on his crew like a race horse pawing at the ground waiting for the pistol to signal the start of the race. Instead I felt more like a horse that had gorged on green apples! These past weeks had been wasted planning and anticipation.

It was no surprise to learn that the Boeing tech reps on the base were so disgusted with our plane that they rejected it. These civilians had the final say on the status of an aircraft. They ascertained that the autopilot couldn't be repaired, and so many things were missing that the decision was made to use it for spare parts. It was permanently grounded and cannibalized. I really believe it was a miracle that we made it safely to England.

They put us gunners with a new pilot, co-pilot, navigator, and bombardier. Our new pilot, Lieutenant Jackson was an officer who had been an instructor pilot and had never seen any action. He enjoyed talking to cadets like they were sub-human, and that's exactly how he approached me.

Lieutenant Jackson stepped into the barracks and shouted, "Come to attention and salute! I'm your new commanding officer."

I had already survived twenty-nine missions on my first tour in the European Theatre. Then I spent weeks working feverishly to help put together a new crew in the States and endured a treacherous trip across the ocean in a slicked up piece of junk only to find out that our comrades were being scattered like marbles. I certainly wasn't in the mood for this. I was lying on my bunk with my arms stretched up and my hands clasped together under my head. After telling him what part of my anatomy he could kiss, I said, "You're not anybody's commanding officer. I won't salute you, and I won't fly with you!" It was obvious where this exchange would take us.

On the way to the major's office, we each carried our attitudes with determination. Lieutenant Jackson told Major Phillips that he wanted to prefer charges against me for insubordination.

The major laughed and said, "Well, you two met and there hasn't been any bloodshed yet?"

I remained at attention while Major Phillips explained to the lieutenant, "This is probably the best flight engineer in the outfit. And you . . . you are a new man at this, not some god in a training camp where you can make the men bow to you."

Feeling justified, I waited to hear who I might be flying with instead. Major Phillips turned to me and said, "The lieutenant is a very good pilot. He *is* your boss, and if I were you, I'd try to get along."

I protested and said, "I'll fly with anyone except him, Sir."

The major sternly said, "No, he needs you real bad and I assure you, he won't attack you again. You two are stuck with each other, so you'd better figure out how to get along. Now, get out!"

The lieutenant and I actually had a talk afterwards. I said, "After you fly a few missions you will understand the difference between training and combat."

Lieutenant Jackson said, "Combat doesn't mean s--- to me! It's discipline that matters." This was a statement that would come back to haunt him.

But give great joy to those who have stood with me in my defense.
Let them continually say,
"Great is the Lord, who enjoys helping his servant."
Psalm 35:27 NLT

OPEN BOMB BAY DOORS – B17G
Vintage Postcard – Courtesy of Anthony Seebaran.
anthony.seebaran@rogers.com

Death Sentence

Lieutenant Jackson and I finally got together somewhat. At least we could speak to each other when necessary. We took off for Germany, and I was so uneasy that I could hardly contain myself. Our co-pilot was a young officer and inexperienced, but I had a feeling he had some grit. I believed he could be trusted, and I knew Jackson could not. At the first sign of danger, I figured Jackson would come apart like an exploding grenade. We would soon find out.

Things were still calm as we flew closer to our destination. We hadn't seen any fighters or gone through any flak yet. Approaching the target, we could now see the flak. It wasn't close to us and wasn't even heavy yet. Lieutenant Jackson screamed and turned loose of the controls! A similar scenario had been running through my head, but the reality was much worse.

The co-pilot grabbed the stick and I asked him, "Can you handle it, sir?"

He chuckled and with a calm voice said, "If you can handle Lieutenant Jackson."

I grabbed Jackson's arm and pulled his mike off so the crew couldn't hear what was happening. Pointing my .45 at his head, I said, "If you don't settle down, I'm going to have to kill you."

Lieutenant Jackson covered his face and wept like a baby. It took him about an hour to calm down. He finally regained his composure, giving me the opportunity to remind him, "Combat doesn't mean s--- to you! Right, Lieutenant Jackson?"

I turned to the co-pilot and asked, "Can you take over at the target and fly through it every mission?" He assured me that he could.

Then I asked the co-pilot, "Are you going to report this incident?"

He said, "I won't, if you and Jackson don't."

Lieutenant Jackson couldn't afford to talk about what had happened – every man on board had heard him scream and knew he had lost it.

I glared at Jackson and requested, "Will you let the co-pilot fly through the flak?" He agreed to this arrangement and nothing more was said on the trip back to Debach Field, England.

Back at the base, I could hardly rest knowing that our crew would be flying with this lunatic again and wondering if we would be able to escape a death sentence next time.

Lord, have mercy on me. See how I suffer
at the hands of those who hate me.
Snatch me back from the jaws of death.
Psalm 9:13 NLT

Heavies Rock Kiel for 2nd Day, Pound Hamburg and Airfields

German naval installations were again plastered by 8th Air Force bombs yesterday. Roughly half of a force of some 1,000 Fortresses and Liberators swung in over Kiel to attack U-boat yards there, while the remainder of the force hit submarine pens at Hamburg and lashed at airfields in northwest Germany.

It marked the second day in a row that Kiel had been hit and the third time in the last six days that the heavies poured it on Nazi naval bases. Two of the last six days, incidentally, were non-operational for the 8th.

(The London Daily Express reported Monday in a dispatch from Stockholm that it is believed there that the Germans in the last two months have been speeding experiments in launching V-weapons from ships and large U-boats, adding that a sub sunk off Bergen, Norway, in February, was believed to have been involved in such experiments.)

Approximately 850 Mustangs and Thunderbolts escorted the heavies and met determined opposition from small numbers of enemy fighters, mostly jet-propelled Me262s, which struck at formations of Liberators. The fighters knocked down 15 Jerries, 11 of them jets, and got eight more in strafing attacks on airfields, but not before some of the Libs were tumbled from the skies.

Nine bombers and four fighters failed to return from the overall operations.

The fighters slashed at the Libs singly and in groups of four and eight, and at least one fighter pilot, Capt. Nile C. Greer, of Blackford, Ky., reported them using the prevailing heavy clouds as a screen. He reported trouble finding the jets in the overcast, but caught one coming out of a cloud and applied the KO at 5,000 feet.

A Lib tail gunner from Minneapolis, Sgt. Calvin W. Mattson, reported that two jets zoomed at his plane from the rear, but neither showed any ability to maneuver as he and other gunners blazed away from all parts of the ship. He reported one as a probable kill.

Thick clouds over most targets necessitated bombing by instrument, and flak was intense to moderate all the way. One gunner coming back after a run over a

(continued on back page)

MAR-10-1945?

THE STARS AND STRIPES
Daily Newspaper for U.S. Armed Forces – European Theater of Operations New York, N.Y. – London, England

168

Combat in the Cockpit

On our next flight, those that could see from their station on the B-17 had a rare and privileged opportunity to witness Patton and the men of the 3rd Army in action.

When I was flying my first tour of missions, each pilot and his crew would have a plane designated to them. Each time a team left the runway, they were in an aircraft that they were familiar with, and the engineer knew what mechanical issues might develop during flight. This second tour was different.

After learning that the crews we had formed were being split, the officials also noted that we would know which plane we would be flying the day of the mission and not before. It was nearing the end of the war. Many planes had been lost or were beyond repair, and they were being replaced with new ones – like the ones our group had flown to England. It must have been strategically better for crew chiefs and their mechanics to repair planes as they came in and simply pull whichever aircraft was cleared first for the next flight crew. I do know that the best technicians and mechanics available were working on those planes. There was never any doubt about that.

We prepared for our next mission, and after a thorough check of the B-17 we took off for our target. Lieutenant Jackson and his co-pilot were at the controls, and we were getting close to enemy territory. Gunners were in their turrets waiting for the call to duty. At this point it seemed that we would have a normal mission. The conflict of piloting the plane through combat action was settled. At least a plan was in place this time.

Then we got our first glimpse of fighting far below us. We had a ringside seat, but this was no sporting event. It was a rare privilege to witness the distinguished Patton and his men as they plowed through enemy territory. Visible to us were tanks firing at each other, artillery lobbing shells, and clouds of dark smoke. And most assuredly from all this action, there would be a blanket of shrapnel covering the entire area. The battle stretched on for at least thirty miles, I know, but probably more like forty or fifty miles. We seemed to be shielded from the war, but in the next moment we would have our own battle in the air.

In the middle of observing Patton and the 3rd Army making history, our awe suddenly turned to terror. Something went wrong and all four engines died almost simultaneously.

Just as I was climbing out of the top turret to investigate the problem, Lieutenant Jackson screamed into the microphone, "Put on your chutes and bail out!"

Knowing that we were in a most critical location, I pushed my mike button and said with confidence, "Don't anybody bail out! There is a battle going on under us and you'll be killed! There's nothing wrong with the engines that I can't fix. Co-pilot, keep us in a glide while I get the engines started."

Jackson shouted, "Are you taking my airplane away from me?"

I said, "Yes I am!"

The electronic controls each had a one-amp fuse, and I found that all fuses had blown. As quickly as possible I changed the four fuses; each time the new fuse was in place, the corresponding engine came back on line.

Immediately after the crisis was over I heard Jackson say to the co-pilot, "Now, you've done it! You forcibly took my airplane!"

The steady young co-pilot didn't even respond. He had a plane to fly.

With my .45 drawn I moved over to the cockpit. I pointed the gun at Jackson and said, "Don't blame him. You know damn well I'm the one that took over the plane! Keep your trap shut and let him fly. We still have a mission to complete."

He was hotter than a branding iron, and there was nothing he could do but sit and smolder. And that's exactly what he did as we flew to our target and the bombs were dropped.

After completing the mission and returning to base, Lieutenant Jackson was chomping at the bit. He couldn't wait to drag me to operations. He knew that he would get no sympathy from the squadron commanding officer, Major Phillips. So Jackson took me to the colonel of operations.

The colonel was one of the few officers I had ever seen that I was about half afraid of. Jackson went in and reported me while I awaited my fate in the adjacent room. The colonel opened the door, sending the lieutenant out and calling me in. I clicked my heels and saluted him, motivated by fear as much as respect.

"Your pilot tells me that you pulled your pistol on him and took over the plane and he was treated like a prisoner on his own ship. Do you want to tell me your side of the story, sergeant?"

I replied, "No, sir. I heard his report to you. He told it the way it happened, sir."

I was holding my breath when I heard this statement from the bird colonel: "I am truly sorry that we have officers who just can't cut it. If you hadn't taken over the aircraft, no doubt some of you would have been killed."

I couldn't figure out how this bird colonel knew so much about what was going on that he sided with me on the incident. He called Lieutenant Jackson back into his office and wanted to talk with both of us.

I said, "Sir, I'll fly with anyone, but not him."

The colonel said, "No, I want you to continue flying with this man."

It was like rewinding and replaying a tape. By now I should have learned my protest carried no weight. Maybe I should have tried a different approach.

The colonel continued, "You two know each other. Lieutenant, you listen to what this sergeant says because he is the flight engineer, and he has plenty of combat experience."

I felt about two-inches tall. His confidence in me was humbling, but I didn't need his implied compliment; I needed out!

Then the colonel said, "Now shake hands and try to get along. Dismissed!"

Dismissed, I thought to myself? That's all, that's the end of it? I should have been thanking God that I wasn't thrown into the stockade and given a court-martial. But at that moment I wasn't sure which was worse: prison or flying with Lieutenant Jackson. It made me wonder what on earth this pilot had on everybody else that kept him from being grounded at the very least. Or, better yet, who was this man kin to? I just couldn't bring myself to believe that it was simply a matter of being short of qualified pilots.

I can't find words to describe how I hated flying combat with this guy, and I have no doubt that he resented me as much. We flew a total of six missions together. Each time, the pilot had the same reaction to flak bursting around us. He always covered his face until things were calm again. The co-pilot did a good job of flying through the flak and over the targets. During all these missions we never experienced what I considered to be heavy flak.

Orders were then handed down canceling any further missions. There would be too much danger of hitting our own men as Patton and the 3rd Army was moving into the heart of Germany. It was a relief not to be flying with Jackson, but it was hard just sitting around knowing that many of our men were still in German prison camps.

Commit everything you do to the Lord.
Trust him, and he will help you.
He will make your innocence as clear as the dawn,
and the justice of your cause will shine like the noonday sun.
Psalm 37:5-6 NLT

BOMBS AWAY
USAAF PHOTO – O. F. Lindsey's Personal Collection

8th Fighters Add 200 To Bag of Nazi Planes

APR. 17 4̸5̸

Fighters of the 8th Air Force continued to ram home the finishing punches td their apparently defenseless, beaten foe, the Luftwaffe, when more than 850 Thunderbolts and Mustangs, which covered approximately 1,000 Liberators and Fortresses on forays deep into southern Germany and Czechoslovakia yesterday, bagged another 200 grounded enemy aircraft.

Thus, the two-day toll taken by the fighters climbed to 941 and set the number put out of action in the last nine days at 1,651. Since Continent-based fighters and bombers have accounted for hundreds more at the same time, the Luftwaffe has in this period received what looks like a mortal blow.

Associated Press reported yesterday from SHAEF that the Luftwaffe's strength had been estimated recently at 4,000 planes. Since Apr. 8, then, Allied fighters had destroyed roughly half this number. And, as a USSTAF staff officer indicated yesterday, the blows against the German Air Force will go on daily at the same terrific tempo.

Accentuating the statement by Gen. Carl Spaatz, USSTAF commander, that the strategic war is over and U.S. air operations will now be designed strictly for cooperation with ground forces, this official declared that every parked German plane is a potential threat to advance Allied columns and must be put out of the way. He said many of the planes destroyed in Monday's record kill of 741 were one- and two-engined fighters, capable of raising hob once they get off the ground.

The bombers also marked the transition to all-out tactical warfare by ranging deep into the shrinking Nazi corridor at the southern end of the fronts to pound three railway centers in Dresden and five rail junctions and an underground oil storage depot in Czechoslovakia.

The junctions were at Kladno, Beraun, Karlsbad, Falkenau and Aussig, and the depot at Roudnice, all near Prague. Four jet-propelled Nazi fighters made a weak stab at one formation of heavies but were driven off immediately by the U.S. fighters.

ROUDNICE=CZ.

THE STARS AND STRIPES
Daily Newspaper for U.S. Armed Forces – European Theater of Operations New York, N.Y. – London, England

Mission of Mercy

After General Patton and the 3rd Army reached the heart of Germany all combat missions were cancelled. Because of this we had some days where there was nothing to do but sit around. We were given three-day passes to London. Several of us shared the use of a bicycle, and I rode it every place nearby, but nothing stopped the anxious feelings or frustration of being grounded. Many gunners were able to transfer to the infantry, and I tried to do the same. But I learned that radio operators and flight engineers were not being accepted.

After a halt in the action and not being allowed to serve in any other capacity, I was really getting anxious. Then one day orders came down for another mission. Our destination would be the Schiphol Airfield of Amsterdam, which had been taken over by the Germans when they invaded Holland.

This site had been the target of repeated bombings by the USAAF and the RAF to force the Luftwaffe out of operation. Now, it was the target of a totally different mission. We were going to fly food to the Dutch. Many of these people had starved to death, and even the Germans occupying the land were starving.

Four hundred B-17's would be flying on this mission, but first they had to be prepared for the special task. We installed wooden platforms constructed to fit into the bomb bay and hang from the bomb racks. Then about a ton of packaged food was put on top of the platforms.

We were given specific instructions detailing the plan. Guns were removed from the turrets. Our commanders didn't want these huge planes sporting .50 calibers to cause concern for civilians or put the enemy on edge. The guns were left inside the planes where they could be quickly retrieved in case of a surprise attack.

We dropped leaflets explaining that the food was to be shared with everyone, and that even the enemy must not be refused his portion. The Germans specifically were warned that if they interfered with the distribution of food in any way, they would be held accountable.

Strangely enough, our formations were being escorted by German pilots flying Messerschmitts that the US forces had captured and disarmed. These German prisoners understood that their own soldiers were starving to death and that food was being dropped for both the Dutch people and the Germans occupying the area. There was no benefit for the German ground troops not to cooperate, although I heard of at least one account in which a B-17 was fired upon.

On approach of the "target," we would be coming in low with our wheels and flaps down to make as slow of a drop as possible. We would then literally "bomb" the target with the food drop. That's all there was to it. No artillery or flak, no fighter attacks, and no destruction, just drop the payload and head for home.

Unfortunately, on the first day of humanitarian aide, packages were bursting open on impact, sending puffs of white smoke into the air from sacks of wheat flour, sugar, and tins of powdered milk. What a royal mess! The Dutch people had gathered out in the open by the thousands to watch and wait for the drop. There were no casualties to my knowledge, which was a miracle in itself as some people were dangerously close to the falling cargo.

It may not have been the most successful run, but it was a mission of mercy, and to show their appreciation the Dutch had a wonderful offering waiting for us. In huge letters, which seemed to stretch out for at least twenty feet in length, were the words "THANKS YANKS" made with beautiful tulips and other flowers. It was all they had to offer, and it was all we could have wanted. How the sight lifted our hearts after months of grueling conditions and tragic losses.

The next day we flew again. This time our cargo was packaged much better and included more different types of food, such as bacon and butter. Some people had not eaten for as long as a month and couldn't tolerate these foods. They could eat crackers, though, and we dropped tons of them, as well.

This operation lasted for six days. Each time, we had four hundred airplanes filled with cargo, and each time, the people came out in droves to greet us. We were later told that the German guards did help distribute the food, and everyone was fed. This was one of the most rewarding times in my military service.

B17s and RAF Bombers Give Holland More Food

Approximately 400 8th Air Force B17s and 500 RAF bombers dropped several hundred tons of food yesterday to beleaguered Dutch civilians in the areas of Alkmaar, Amsterdam, Hilversum and Utrecht.

Duplicating Tuesday's operation, Forts of the 3rd Air Division slung another 800 tons of 10-in-1 rations from tree-top heights. Grateful Hollanders, using rocks and wood, spelled out "Thank You" signs around the drop zones.

APRIL 3, 1945

THE STARS AND STRIPES

Daily Newspaper for U.S. Armed Forces – European Theater of Operations New York, N.Y. – London, England

God blesses those who are hungry and thirsty for justice,
for they will receive it in full.
Matthew 5:6 NLT

Victory in Europe

Soon V.E. Day came. Victory in Europe, what a grand occasion! There was celebrating and shooting everywhere. A lieutenant shot my good friend, Captain Ice, in the arm – not nearly fatal, but so senseless. A sergeant shot another soldier, but I did not see the incident. I never did learn if it was a serious injury. But then, anytime a person is shot with a .45, it's almost always serious.

Major Phillips saw that I was sober and ordered me to help him disarm everyone. We filled knapsacks with .45's and they were heavy. We found a master sergeant hiding, trying to keep his gun. When Major Phillips demanded he turn over his weapon, he insisted that he didn't have one.

His hands were behind his back as I approached him to take the gun by force. I heard a loud bang, saw a flash behind him, and then he screamed. I had the flashlight on him and saw something fly from him, but it didn't appear to be an ejected cartridge case. With all the noise around us I couldn't be sure if the bang had come from a gun, let alone his gun.

I picked up the dropped gun and removed the magazine. Then I pulled the slide back expecting to eject a live round, and out popped a spent cartridge. The slide was blocked enough that it did not automatically reload. Looking in the grass, I found his finger, which had been completely blown off his hand by the blast. We summoned help to get this drunk carried to the infirmary.

Finally, things settled down. When everyone was sober, they remembered that I was the one taking guns. I was surprised that no one gave me any grief over it. This was such a great, God-given victory, and here some people had to celebrate by getting drunk and shooting each other.

We should be decent and true in everything we do, so that everyone can approve of our behavior. Don't participate in wild parties and getting drunk,
or in adultery or immoral living, or in fighting and jealousy.
Romans 13:13 NLT

The Flight Home

Finally, after days of waiting around at Headquarters, we loaded up our B-17's and took off for the States. We basically traced, in reverse, the same route that we flew when we came to England – stopping in Iceland, Greenland, etc. for refueling and other needs.

As we began our flight, it wasn't long before talk turned to the subject of women. The guys kidded me that I had a girl in every country. In England there had been lots of opportunities for me to build a reputation. There were so many eligible women in London that no one had trouble getting a date. Because of the war almost everything was rationed, and all prices were controlled. This meant meals, drinks, and even shows were very affordable. A guy could take a young lady out and show her a really good time.

One comrade pushed the issue and asked, "Well, what about it, Tex? Do you have a girl in every country?"

I said, "Sure I have, even in Iceland."

My crew chief said, "Now, I've been there, and there *are* no women. In fact, I'll bet you ten dollars you can't show me a girl there that knows you.

Looking around at the guys I said, "OK, I'll take that bet."

We landed at Reykjavik, secured the airplane, and then went to chow. Afterwards I said, "Let's go to the Red Cross and have a cup of coffee."

My crew chief said, "Yeah, I want to see this girlfriend of yours."

When we walked in, Cele was behind the counter. She saw us come in and ran to meet me. She gave me a big hug and a kiss. I said, "Cele, do you remember my name?"

With a smile she answered, "You're Oral Lindsey." When the ole sarge heard my name, he knew he had just lost ten dollars.

Cele had a big laugh and then told the sarge that she always remembers names. We had spent a lot of time together during that one stopover, but we never developed a relationship. We were just good friends.

Now the sergeant really had all the guys giving me a hard time about the girls. He said, "He's the sorriest looking guy in the outfit. Why on earth do women go for him?"

I told him, "While you guys are waiting around for a girl to come over and talk to you, I'm already asking the girl for a date. If she turns me down, I just brush off my pride and ask another girl if she is interested in going with me."

Contrary to what these men thought, there were other things on my mind besides women. I was wondering about my future with military, my family at home, and what other opportunities I might explore.

Back in the States we went through processing, interrogation, and were issued furloughs. After all the red tape most of us bought tickets for the train or a bus that would take us home for a long awaited reunion. Along the way I met up with my old pilot, Major Glenn, and he said, "Let's try it once more. Let's go to the B-29's and you can be my engineer. We'll go fight the Japs."

I gladly accepted the invitation. We went to San Antonio, Texas, together and were working toward that goal when V. J. day came – Victory in Japan!

It was not like Victory in Europe. V.J. was not an unconditional surrender. In fact the number one villain, Hirohito, was not touched at all. And I don't believe all his murderous leaders were ever brought to justice.

However, this treaty was the best that we could have expected. I believed it was the right thing for our country to accept it.

In Japan the emperor was considered to be a god. Every Japanese soldier and civilian would have died to protect him. It would take a long time before the people of Japan realized that they had been lied to and were just being used by their leaders.

With the war already over in Europe and now in the Pacific, it wasn't long before I received my discharge papers. I stayed in the reserves knowing that I would probably return and make a career of the military.

For now, though, I was taking a year off. There were a lot of things in my home town to catch up on, and I was ready to live a little!

... "No eye has seen, no ear has heard, and no mind has imagined what God has prepared for those who love him."
I Corinthians 2:9 NLT

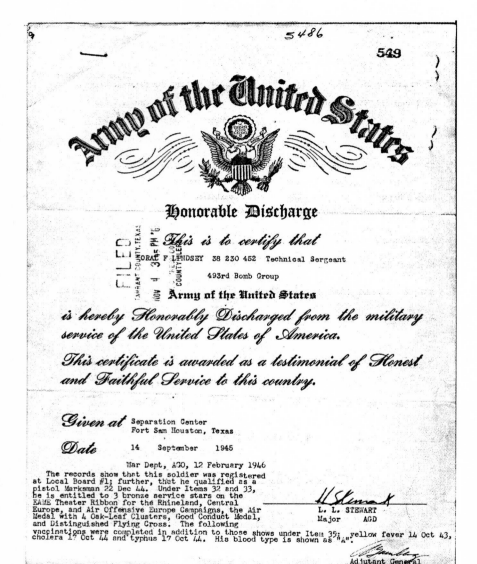

5486

549

Army of the United States

Honorable Discharge

This is to certify that

ORAL F LINDSEY 38 230 452 Technical Sergeant

493rd Bomb Group

Army of the United States

FILED
TARRANT COUNTY, TEXAS
NOV 4 3 ½ 5 PM '46
COUNTY CLERK ... COUNTY

is hereby Honorably Discharged from the military service of the United States of America.

This certificate is awarded as a testimonial of Honest and Faithful Service to this country.

Given at Separation Center
Fort Sam Houston, Texas

Date 14 September 1945

War Dept, AGO, 12 February 1946

The records show that this soldier was registered at Local Board #1; further, that he qualified as a pistol Marksman 22 Dec 44. Under Items 32 and 33, he is entitled to 3 bronze service stars on the EAME Theater Ribbon for the Rhineland, Central Europe, and Air Offensive Europe Campaigns, the Air Medal with 4 Oak-Leaf Clusters, Good Conduct Medal, and Distinguished Flying Cross. The following vaccinations were completed in addition to those shows under Item 35; yellow fever 14 Oct 43, cholera 17 Oct 44 and typhus 17 Oct 44. His blood type is shown as "A".

L. L. STEWART
Major   AGD

Adjutant General

186

Personal Letters

Introduction

Through their correspondence we get a personal look into the hearts and minds of soldier, family, and friends enduring separation and the trials of war.

A portion of each letter is pictured followed by a typed copy of the entire correspondence for easier reading.

A Letter from Home

Stamford, Texas Dec 26th 1944
Our Dear hero we got your sweet
interesting letter this eaving
about two thirty oclock
seem like the mail man
never would come The roads
were So sleek an icey, we was
So glad and thankfull too
that you was well and
geting some rest & shut
eye glad you saw the Kr.
about your self, hope he dident
eat you out,, papa caughs
pretty hard Sometimes he is
better he's asleep now and its
nearly 9 oclock and he dident
caugh any hardly when he lay
down, its so cold & disaqueely
out doors missting rain &
most of it freezes on the
grown when it hits its driping
off the house now so it
must be turning warmer

December 26, 1944
Stamford, Texas

Our Dear Hero

We got your sweet interesting letter this eaving about two thirty oclock. Seem like the mailman never would come. The roads were so sleek and icey. We was so glad and thankful too that you was well and getting some rest & shut-eye. Glad you saw the Dr. about your self, hope he didn't eat you out, Papa coughs pretty hard. Sometimes he is better. He's asleep now and it's nearly 9 oclock and he didn't cough any hardly when lay down. It's so cold & disagreebly out doors misting rain & most of it freezes on the ground when it hits. It's dripping off the house now so it must be turning warmer.

Papa has tried to take care of his self all he could. When he goes out he can keep his feet dry & warm & that helps alot. I told him to be very careful and stay in the house all he can. He said, well I mean to. He had to go to town this morning to mail you your box of candy. Arvin told him yesterday to be sure and mail it so Oral will get in plenty time. He (**Papa**) said he never got cold, only his face. He had on his cap, over shoes, over coat and gloves, ha ha. But the fine rain was peppering down.

I am fine as can be. I hope I don't take Pa's cold. We think it's awful if we get alittle out doors or in a car, and to think what our men & boy heros are going through with. We wonder how any of them are living, go where it would kill a brute. It's so cold and come down and go back and do the same thing the next day.

Son, Papa and me got the prettiest Christmas Card today from T/Sgt Roy Bevins, it was from him & his wife. He is in Denver, Col. I can't make out his address...

You may no right where he is. He said on the card he was Oral's left waist crew ha ha. That's the best I can make it out ha ha.

I told Papa I wish Nellie was here I no She can read it alrite and Arvin is pretty good. I am poor hand to read a strange handwrite unless it's very plain. And dear we got a card from Lona & B. C. today. She said she was feeling alrite but B.C.s heart was bothering him worse the day she wrote her card. That was the 22nd. She mailed it that day too and your letter was wrote 22nd and mailed 23rd. See if it hadn't been Sunday we would have got Lona's card Monday. If it hadn't been Christmas Day ha ha. But there were too many if's in the way.

Lona said I hope you have herd from Punk (Oral) since he went back and I wonder if he got the pk we sent him. She said she never insured it and he may not get it. I have her a letter on the way and I told her Oral got her pk and Clyde's too and I wrote Clyde the same. So they would no. Oh, I'm a pretty good phone Switch ha ha. I just Switch the news to everyone ha ha. I should be good for something. I'm not good for nothing that I can see.

This war news would run any person crazy that had an ounce of sence. Very idea our air boys killing over a thousand of our boys that the Germans captured the other day. They dropped bombs on the place where they had them corralled & where the wounded ones were too. And the Germans said our boys killed all of them. Some of them were British men and some were French I think. This is what the Germans are telling but it could be true.

Old Hitler was three months planning this battle and he really done a good job of it, if they want to no what I think a bout it. He out numbers our army two to one on every front or flank and I am like you I don't see any end to this war in sight.

I believe you get more letters from Marine than you do from Pa and me ha ha. I bet those boys in the baricks worry you or do they have more corrospondants than you? No news only Bad war news. So I'll go to bed.

Wednesday morning 27th – Papa feels better this morning. He never sleep very much last nite but he's not coughing near so bad. I feel fine, and I pray Oral feels well for he has an awful hard and frightful job ahead of him. It almost the flesh on my bones pries off to think about you going right back in this toughest part. But I am praying that God will protect you & bring you home as he did before.

Pearl had for her Christmas guest her soldier Son, Arvel that has been over seas 18 months. He hardly can walk, he is wounded in one foot and has a spinal trouble. The wound affected a nerve that went to his back. He had been in a hospital over there some place for three weeks. His nephew came same time he did. He has a bullet wound clear through his head. Went through one temple & out at the other. He had his right mind when he came last Thursday. But he went crazy before Christmas Day and they had to take him back to the hospital in Temple Texas. He has a wife and they live at Hamlin, Texas.

Honey I don't care if you get old Hitler on your first mission and if you did the whole world ought to bow down to you ha ha. I am getting gone and don't have nothing worth telling, lots love and good luck and may God's richest blessings rest upon you and your buddies – Your Papa and Mama

A Soldier's Reply

(P.1) January 13th 1944

Dear mama and papa I'm fine,
just got back from London. I
was paid the other day and got
a pass the same day so we took
off for London. Al, Roy and I
went through Westminister-
Abby and saw a lot of the
sights in different parts of
the town. M. Abby is an old
Church that was built before
the eleventh century. We
saw the tomb of 26 Monks
in the Church and a lot of
small tombs. And we saw about
a million things that I could
tell you about but it's hard

(Written to his parents in January 1944 during his first tour in Europe.)

Oral F. Lindsey

January 13, 1944

Dear Mama and Papa

I'm fine, I just got back from London. I was paid the other day and got a pass the same day so we took off for London. Al, Roy, and I went through Westminster Abby and saw a lot of the sights in different parts of the town. W. Abby is an old church that was built before the eleventh century. We saw the tomb of 26 monks in the church and lot of small tombs. And we saw about a million things that I could tell you about but it's hard to put on paper.

I'm sending you $200.00 that I don't need. I owe $17.00 tythe and you can take care of that for me and send Lona $10. for me. I'll have $28 after I send this and it's not many days until I get paid again. Use what you need of this and buy bonds with the other.

In case you'd like to know why I had that much money, I'll tell you. I got some back pay that I didn't get two months ago. .....

I got a letter from Ann mailed Dec. 30th and one from Arvin dated Dec. 17th. If you write Ann tell her I've got six letters from her I think. I'll try to write her first chance but I write to so many different ones that I'm usually late writing to everyone.

I got your letter telling about Christmas and sure wish I could have been there. I'm glad you had a good Christmas dinner and saw most of the children. Write me when you get this.

I'll write again soon and maybe I'll more in the mood, ha ha. Tell the children to keep writing.

Love and Best Wishes, Oral

An English Lady Writes

Friday 24-11-44.

My Dear Oral,

many thanks for your very nice letter I received today, written 22-10-44.

yes I did write to you while I was in London, I wish you had of been there too, you could have met my friends Mr & Mrs. ———, they treat me like a daughter.

Mr. ——— wrote to you to see if you could get him any zip partners, I hope you don't mind, I suggested it; he makes leather hand bags for a hobby, but the steel leather partners are very scarce. I hope you do get back

200

4

curtains, just so that the
lights are not too bright.
I went to the cinema last
night to see James Cagney in
The Oklahoma Kid it was
jolly good, I love cow-boy
films.

I have not heard from
Dave for over a fortnight, he
was in Holland last time I
heard from him.

Do you remember the badges
and needle you gave me, I still
have them.

Well Oral, have you got a girl
friend yet or are you just keeping
along like me, I have not seen
Dave since last xmas, I
met him last xmas eve while

NR Stone

Staffs

England

Friday 24-11-44

My Dear Oral,

Many thanks for your very nice letter I received today written 22-10-44.

Yes I did write to you while I was in London, I wish you had of been there too, you could have met my friends Mr. & Mrs.Cxxxxx they treat me like a daughter.

Mr. Cxxxxx wrote to you to see if you could get him any zip fasteners. I hope you don't mind, I suggested it, he makes leather hand bags for a hobby but the steel fasteners are very scarce.

I hope you do get back to England, I should love to see you again. We will have a lot to talk about. How is your Mom? I hope she is well, I have written to her again.

I hope you all have a very happy Christmas. I will be thinking of you and hoping you are at home. Well dear the country side is bare now, we seem to have rain every day too, there are no leaves and no flowers. I will be glad when the Spring comes again.

I am still filling depth charges and bombs, my hands are awfully yellow and the front of my hair is zinged (what a mess). We are all in this together.

I may be having a photo of myself to send you soon that's if it's good. I had my photo taken last week at a friends house. My Auntie likes your photo ever so much and so do I. It is in a frame on my dressing table now.

There are hardly any lights on in London yet, because if there is a raid they have to black out again in a hurry. My friends don't draw their black out curtains, we must have some kind of curtains, just so that the lights are not too bright.

I went to the cinema last night to see James Cagney in The Oklahoma Kid! It was jolly good, I love cow-boy films.

I have not heard from Dave for over a fortnight, he was in Holland last time I heard from him. **(Dave is her brother.)**

Do you remember the badges and needles you gave me, I still have them. Well Oral, have you got a girl friend yet or are you just trudging along like me. I have not seen Dave since last Christmas, I met him last Christmas eve while I was on leave, then I came back here and we have not met since.

I am on early morning shift this week and we have to be up for 5 am. We only have tomorrow then we start nights on Sunday at 10 PM.

I am glad President Roosevelt has been elected again, he seems to know how to run things also he has helped us a lot. Did you vote?

Well I will close now hoping you and your friends are well, hoping to hear from you very soon.

Good night. Lots of Love and Best of Luck

Joyce xxxxx

Here is a wee verse, written how we talk at home, I hope you can read it.

May your heart be free from care,
May you aye have gear to spare,
May your out-look aye be fair,
Though crops seem failin;

-                -   -

May your troubles aye be few,
May your freen's be ever true,
May your meal-poke aye be full,
Your kail-pot skailin.

Wishing you a very merry Christmas.

Expressions of Gratitude
Never Faded

Introduction

While conducting photo research for the publication of this work a message board was discovered with postings from individuals around the world regarding WWII and the Allied Forces. Several messages noted a sincere desire to thank those allied soldiers that helped put an end to Hitler's tyranny.

We contacted those that were appropriate and offered them the opportunity to write a letter expressing their gratitude and asked permission to publish them. In this section we have included four such letters.

Mr. Lindsey was overwhelmed with the stories these private citizens had to share and desires to personally write each individual. He also wanted to say "Thank You" publicly in this section of *Top Turret*.

We offer our sincere apologies to anyone whose letter did not reach us.

From Belgium

and whenever some of them, shot down and rescued by the "terrorists" - as the nazi called them - were hidden in my uncle's farm, I tried to meet them, to see them, to talk to them; but it was to no avail: who would trust unto a 5 years old, the knowledge of the existence next door of people that were searched for by the Germans?

Now that I eventually can come in direct contact with one of them, the occasion is there to express my gratitude to all these men through one of them. Such a (60 years long) longing to tell them, that eventually comes to its end, causes me such an emotion that my tears flow from my eyes down to this paper. What else can I say than Thank you, thank you, thanks to all of you. You did not do it in vain. And, PLEASE, be sure to stop by at my place if you come to the D-Day celebrities - or send your children or grandchildren at any time, you are welcome, they are welcome.

Hans

Francis Baudoux   June 2004

Vieux Genappe

Belgium

Dear Mr. Lindsey

I am looking forward to reading the book you have in printing about your experience as a WWII Airman. This is because I have had for the most important part of my life a big interest into the life and the difficulties of these brave young men that were flying over my head when I was 5 to 7 years old in Nazis occupied Belgium.

At that time I was not particularly unhappy when compared to the majority of persons. Neither a Jewish boy nor a poor city boy, I assume that I was living the decent life of a somewhat wealthy country family. Food was available at a price my Mother could pay – she earned enough as an MD but my father was away, POW in German camps. Although I hardly knew him – I was less than two years old when he had to go at war as a reserve cavalry Belgian Army – I was missing him tremendously. And my Mother kept telling me everyday, "Soon the Americans will come, and your Father is going to be freed, and he will come back."

So whenever allied airplanes were flying over our village I was mentally thanking them for coming, and risking their life every minute of their overflight for my own benefit. I was trembling for them and whenever some of them were shot down and rescued the "terrorists" – as the Nazis called them – were hidden in my uncle's farm, I tried to meet them, to see them, to talk to them, but it was to no avail. Who would trust unto a five-year old the knowledge of the existence nextdoor of people that were searched for by the Germans?

Now that I eventually can come in direct contact with one of them, the occasion is there to express my gratitude to all these men through one of them. Such a (sixty years long) longing to tell them, that eventually comes to its end, causes me such an emotion that tears flow from my eyes down to this paper. What else can I say than thank you, thank you, thanks to all of you.

You did not do it in vain. And, please be sure to stop by at my place if you come to the D-Day Celebrations or send your children or grandchildren at anytime, you are welcome, they are welcome.

Francis

Peaceful Retirement

A Happy Ending – Aerial View of Village

Jean Baudoux, when released by Allied armies from a German POW camp, returned to Belgium where he later became an officer in the Belgian Air Force. He and his wife spent their retirement in the village – after a few years as Public Relations Officer of a US corporation during which years he especially enjoyed the company of many American colleagues – Some of them kept visiting him there from Illinois, until he died in 1992.

School Boy Daze
England

MR E.T JONES
80 EDGECOMB RD
STOWMARKET
SUFFOLK
IP14 2DW

DEAR ORAL

I WAS BORN IN 1934 AND LIVED IN STOWMARKET SUFFOLK.

WE WERE SURROUNDED BY AIRFIELDS, FIRST RAF THEN USAF.

REMEMBER EARLY PART OF WAR WITH THE FIGHTERS AND THEN THE BOMBERS. IT IS A WONDER WE LEARNT ANYTHING AT SCHOOL, SPENT MOST OF THE DAY LOOKING OUT OF THE CLASSROOM WINDOW OR WHEN THE SIREN SOUNDED IN THE SHELTERS.

WE USED TO BIKE OUT TO THE AIRFIELDS AFTER SCHOOL TO WATCH THEM REFUEL AND REARM THE AIRCRAFT, WE HAD DOUBLE SUMMERTIME THEN SO IT DIDNT GET DARK UNTIL 11 PM.

Mr. E. T. Jones
Stowmarket
Suffolk, England

Dear Oral

I was born in 1934 and lived in Stowmarket, Suffolk. We were surrounded by airfields, first RAF then USAAF. Remember early part of war with the fighters and the bombers. It is a wonder we learnt anything at school, spent most of the day looking out of the classroom window or when the siren sounded in the shelters.

We used to bike out to the airfields after school to watch them refuel and re-arm the aircraft. We had double summertime then so it didn't get dark until 11:00 PM. We had fighter and bomber airfields very close to the town, Wattisham and Rattlesden. We used to watch the B-17s, B-24s, P-47s, P-38s, and then the Mustangs.

We had rationing so we were quite hungry. The Americans were very generous. They laid on many parties for us children. Can remember the trucks and the large fuel tankers with their air brakes, a new noise to us. Was a witness to a collision between a tanker and a milk lorry. We were on our way to the swimming pool for lessons. Was cancelled as they used all the water to make foam to put out the fire.

One day I was walking up Poplar Hill, main road to Wattisham Airfield, when this USAAF truck was going up the hill when the tail board fell down and this crate came out and crashed on the road. It broke open and all these cans of dried milk came out. We collected as many as we could and ran home.

Remember how smart the Americans were in their gabardine uniforms. We used to chase after them asking for chewing gum. Can remember refreshers.

I should like to thank you and your comrades for coming to our help when we needed it most. No doubt in my mind we would have been under the Jack Boot without your bravery and efforts.

Yours Thankfully,

Edward Jones

Operation Chowhound
Netherlands

Evert Pieter van Marken

Netherlands

Oral Franklin Lindsay

U.S.A.

2004-06-10

Dear Sir,

A few days ago I watched the D-day commemorations in Normandy on television. The start of the beginning of the end of World War II on June 6 1944 at a terrible cost in lives of so many Allies. The soldiers to whom we owe so much.

On May 2 1945, relief came in the form of B-17 bombers, dropping sacks of food on the airfield of Schiphol. I was there, in a barge in the canal adjoining the airfield collecting the sacks and gorging myself on the contents of some of them which had burst open. I scooped out bacon and butter from broken tins, dipping it in sugar. Everybody else did the same thing. It was absolutely georgeous.

During my research on Internet and after visiting the War Horse website, I came accross my heroes, the men who flew those B-17's in Operation Chowhound, the name given to the food droppings in Holland by the USAAF. Crew members from the 385th Bomb Group. Men like Frank Mays, Bob Silver, Carl Hannon, Harold E. Provence and others, who took the trouble contacting me. I received one e-mail from Jkbmps@ who did not sign his name.

He wrote that he piloted the lead B-17 out of the 549th squadron, 385th Bomb Group, 8th Air Force, Great Ashfield and dropped food over a town called Hilversum.

As Frank May wrote: this electronic world of computers and friends sure is a good thing, sometimes! Frank was a Ball Turret Gunner at the time and was 79 last year. So is Bob Silver, a 1st Pilot at the age of 21. Keeping the memories alive. You were all lucky – or – your Guardian Angels played a big role seeing you through the war and the years afterwards - as Frank Mays also wrote. You are all my heroes to whom we all owe so much.

But you were the invisible heroes. Not like the soldiers who liberated our towns and were warmly welcomed and embraced by the girls and marching in Victory parades. I was afraid for you when your planes flew over at night on the way to Germany. The Flak was dense and noisy and the searchlight beams many. The shrapnel came whizzing down in the night and fell noisily on our roof.

I have tried to convey this to my sons and their sons and I hope I have succeeded.

Thank you, thank you all,.

Sincerely,

Pieter van Marken

Evert Pieter van Marken
Amstelveen
Netherlands

Dear Sir,

A few days ago I watched the D-day commemorations in Normandy on television. The start of the beginning of, the end of WWII on June 6, 1944 at a terrible cost in lives of so many Allies – the soldiers to whom we owe so much.

Late last year my sons asked me to write my life story for them which included the war years and I researched what happened at the end of the war in particular.

I was fifteen years old at the time and lived near the Amsterdam Airport Schiphol, in a town called Amstelveen where I now happen to live again. The airfield was one of the most heavily defended German airfields and was bombed several times by USAAF B-26 Marauders with R.A.F. Spitfire fighter cover in 1943. The Luftwaffe abandoned Schiphol as a result.

Late in 1944, there was a terrible shortage of food in Western Holland. We were cut off from the liberated part of the Netherlands and the Germans had cut off our food supplies. We suffered real hunger during that winter. I cycled for many hours in the bitter cold to beg for food from farmers. A pound of wheat here and a pound there to be ground up to make bread. My mother made cake from tulip bulbs and cooked sugar beets into a horrible tasting porridge. My parents had already bartered their gold wedding rings and our grand piano, for food with greedy farmers to help feed their four children.

On May 2nd 1945 relief came in the form of B-17 Bombers dropping sacks of food on the airfield of Schiphol. I was there, in a barge in the canal adjoining the airfield collecting the sacks and gorging myself on the contents of some of them which had burst open. I scooped out bacon and butter from broken tins, dipping it in sugar. Everybody else did the same thing. It was absolutely gorgeous.

During my research on Internet and after visiting the War Horse website, I came across my heroes, the men who flew those B-17s in Operation Chowhound, the name given to the food drop in Holland by the USAAF. Crew members from the 385th Bomb Group. Men like Frank Mays, Bob Silver, Carl Hannon, Harold E. Province, and others, who took the trouble contacting me.

I received one email from jkbmps@cs.com who did not sign his name. He wrote that he piloted the lead B-17 out of the 549th Squadron, 385th Bomb Group, 8th Air Force, Great Ashfield and dropped food over a town called Hilversum.

As Frank May wrote: "This electronic world of computers and friends sure is a good thing, sometimes!" Frank was a ball turret gunner at the time and was 79 last year. So is Bob Silver, a 1st Pilot, at the age of 21. Keeping the memories alive. You were all lucky – or – your guardian Angels played a big role seeing you through the war and the years afterwards – as Frank Mays also wrote. You are all my heroes to whom we all owe so much.

But you were the invisible heroes. Not like the soldiers who liberated our towns and were warmly welcomed and embraced by the girls and marching in Victory parades. I was afraid for you when your planes flew over at night on the way to Germany. The flak was dense and noisy and the search lights many. The shrapnel came whizzing down in the night and fell noisily on our roof.

I have tried to convey this to my sons and their sons and I have succeeded. Thank you, thank you all.

Sincerely,

Pieter van Marken

Watching from Long Thurlow
England

were:
You are welcome to use all of this letter or any part that you feel is relevant. It gives me, as an Englishman, a great honour to write to one of the Americans who helped keep my Grandparents safe, 60 years ago. Without you I wouldn't be here. The best of luck to you sir. All the best.

TIM MEEKINGS.

Bury St. Edmunds
Suffolk, England

Dear Frank,

I didn't have to think long and hard about to write to you. My Granddad has told me many times about Great Ashfield Base and the B-17s giving them an early morning wake-up call. My Granddad worked as an agricultural contractor before, during and after the war, so early morning rises were normal for him.

My Grandparents lived about a mile from the base and heard the explosions when the base was bombed. They saw the American servicemen everyday and have always said that they were very polite.

I visit the airfield whenever possible, because I only live about ten miles away. Standing there looking at what remains of the main runway, it often makes me think of what I would have said to a member of the 385th Bomb Group, if I had met them during their stay there. I'd like to think Frank, that if we had met in 1944, first off I'd have shook your hand and said, "Do you fancy a beer, friend?" Sitting in an English Pub, I would have asked you about life in America.

My parents taught me to be polite and hopefully you'd sense that I was genuine towards you and not just wanting cigarettes and chocolate from a "Yank". My Grandparents have always been church-goers and I know for a fact they would have treated you kindly, possibly inviting you for a cup of tea.

I really do hope that the people you met over here were kind to you, although I doubt they all were.

You are welcome to use all of this letter or any part that you feel is relevant. It gives me, as an Englishman, a great honor to write to one of the Americans who helped keep my Grandparents safe, sixty years ago. Without you I wouldn't be here.

Best of Luck to you, Sir. All the Best.   Tim Meekings

The Rest of the Story

Rated "R" for Graphic Violence

It's impossible to write about events in any war and not remember seeing things that haunt you the rest of your life. Movies are made all the time using special effects to show destruction of the human body in graphic detail.

But there is no way to compare viewing a film with living the tragedy. When you're there, it's more than visually graphic. You experience it physically, mentally, and emotionally, all the while knowing you can't stop the film. You can't walk out – this isn't a theatre, or breathe a sigh of relief – this isn't a film. You live with the sights running through your head and you can't ignore them or gloss over them. Lest we forget that in reality *war is hell,* the two stories that follow make this account of WWII more complete.

I do not remember what the target was on this particular mission. In fact, everything about this day was blotted from my mind by the intensity of a disturbing event. My memory picks up just after leaving a target. We had increased speed and opened up the formation somewhat. There was always someone who would say, "Let's get the hell out of here!"

Nowhere did the enemy fight you like they did right before, during, and immediately after the bomb run. This fifteen-minute segment of an eight to nine-hour flight was the most dangerous. If there was any hatred or anger shown by the Germans, it was at the target, for it was here that the factory, rail yards, airbase, or store houses were bombed or burned.

Right after we left the target, the Messerschmitts came at us hard, and every gun that could reach him was blazing back.

Far ahead I saw fire streaming from an unidentified plane, and then the pilot bailed out. When his chute opened I saw that it was brown, and I felt relief as all of our chutes were white. We were closing on him quickly and by now we were at his elevation. I knew that we would go right by him. At an altitude of 30,000 feet our actual speed was 240 mph, not the 180 mph that the gauge was showing. Then a B-17 flying in formation close to us but higher by about fifty feet suddenly hit the German pilot at his waist. I saw the man's legs swing under the wing and then fall like sticks of wood. The parachute, still open, carried the man's body down.

Bill Clark saw it happen also and later admitted, "I thought I was going to throw up."

It was difficult seeing a man die in such a cruel way. All life is precious, but I admit that I was thankful it wasn't one of our men.

Soon after, on a somewhat similar mission, I would see even worse. The first moment that I was aware of impending disaster was when our left wing man pulled out of formation.

We were just approaching the target, absolutely the worst place to leave formation. I could see the left side of the plane was on fire. The plane was just ahead of us and at a slightly higher altitude. The pilot was maneuvering the plane away to keep from taking us down with him in the event that the plane should explode.

Whatever battle damage they sustained must have caused other problems because suddenly the tail of the plane broke off. I could see the two waist gunners standing there for a second, and then both of them jumped out.

They were falling away from the plane. Then both chutes opened. I don't know if the men pulled the ripcords or if something else triggered them, but the chutes opened too soon after they bailed out. An instant later, the whole B-17 exploded into a ball of fire. The heat was so intense and the parachutes were so close that they caught fire, as well.

Back at the base I didn't read the names posted as missing or killed in action. These were men from my own squadron. By now I had learned that I wasn't strong enough to handle all the tragedies and simply keep going. I always hoped and believed that the tail gunner got out.

*Even the depths of Death and Destruction
are known by the Lord.
How much more does he know the human heart!
Proverbs 15:11 NLT*

The Lost Returned

A friend gave me this simple note requesting that I please hold on to it in case something happened to him. I assured him that I would follow the instructions even though we both knew that officials didn't allow individuals to handle such matters.

I never believed that I would need to give the note another thought. Yet, one day the news came – my friend along with the entire crew were lost in battle. Their plane was seen going down in flames and no parachutes deployed that anyone could see. The official report was "Missing in Action".

Having no authority, I could only stand by while base personnel gathered Tommy's things. They weren't happy with my supervision but I stayed anyway to make sure that all of the items he had listed were picked up. Later, sitting on my bunk, I wrote his mother. She would be receiving an official telegram from the USAAF long before she would get my letter. I was hoping that it might bring her some comfort to read a personal note from a friend of Tommy's.

Duty called and I continued to fly knowing that Tommy was just one of the thousands that were lost and the only thing anyone could do was keep fighting. This is why it was such a burden for us when the war reached the stage that grounded all flights. We knew it was necessary to prevent harm to the 3rd Army now entering the heart of Germany. It was just difficult not being able to fly or help our men in their efforts.

Many years later the 385th held reunions like many other bomb groups. Finally the opportunity came and my wife and I were able to attend one of these gatherings. What an experience it was to see friends, bonded by joy and tragedy.

I heard someone mention Tommy and I commented about the loss of such a fine comrade. Then I was told that he wasn't dead! He had survived and was taken prisoner, but eventually made it home once victory was declared in Europe. Although, we never made contact, I have often thought of the comrade who was lost for a time but then God returned him to his family and friends.

For you have rescued me from death;
you have kept my feet from slipping.
So now I can walk in your presence, oh God,
in your life-giving light.
Psalm 56:13 NLT

Non-Combat Missions

Only flights labeled as "combat" were credited to the required number of missions to complete a tour of duty. Anyone reading this must have already wondered what we did on days that we weren't on a combat mission. I can assure you we were not idle. There were other flights that put us in danger of enemy attack and flights with inherent mechanical failure.

One thing our crew did was fly top secret documents to Valley Wales. We all had top secret clearances but some, like Dick Wheaton, had higher levels of clearance. These missions involved such sensitive documents that Operations would handcuff a locked briefcase to Wheaton's arm for security. We would kid him that if the Germans captured us, they would just cut his arm off and take the brief case. He did not find this humorous.

These missions were very short and were flown with little more than a skeleton crew. We took off from Great Ashfield and just cleared the tree tops climbing on to the required 5,000 feet. By the time we reached that elevation, we would almost immediately begin our descent. This distance was probably around eighty miles or so.

Once at our destination the crew would all leave the plane and go over to the mess hall while Wheaton delivered the briefcase. When the officials released him, he would join us in the mess hall. Sometimes there would be a short layover while return documents were prepared for Wheaton. The pilot would take us back to Great Ashfield after our meal.

In addition to flying secret courier missions, I had become a check-flight engineer. Many planes and entire crews had been lost during my first tour in the European Theatre. I was the only flight engineer in the four squadrons allowed to check-fly the worst airplanes such as those B-17's that had a whole wing change, planes with four new or replaced engines, and those with massive battle damage.

Of course these planes were fairly safe. They had been inspected by tech-reps and civilians with great knowledge of all the systems. We knew our mechanics had a lot of skill and integrity. I trusted them with my life.

On these missions we always flew with a skeleton crew: pilot, co-pilot, flight engineer, and radio operator. All the check-pilots were excellent and had plenty of experience. After making our own inspection we took off and flew anywhere from four to eight hours. I recorded everything that was out of tolerance or failed in any way. I also recorded each engine's performance. We never had a major problem and only found minor discrepancies.

For this service I received nine dollars per diem because it was always done at night. You received per diem when you were not provided food and sleeping quarters. For about three months I flew one of these every night, even when I flew a combat mission. Several times I drew almost $270 per month. That doesn't sound like much today, but back then it was the equivalent of $2700 dollars today.

I finally had to stop pulling this double-duty and get some rest and more sleep. I had lost too much weight and was beginning to feel the effects on my body. At this point I weighed 127 pounds and was six feet tall. That put me in the unhealthy category. But I missed having the job and regretted losing more than half of my pay.

I am grateful for the opportunity to have flown with these men. What an honor it had been.

Be glad for all God is planning for you.
Be patient in trouble, and always be prayerful.
Romans 12:12 NLT

Inside the Top Turret

Since the top turret is such an important part of this book, I'd like to explain more about it. It was properly called a Sperry Upper-Local Turret. The gun carriage held two Browning, .50 caliber, air-cooled machine guns. It rotated freely a full 360 degrees azimuth and almost 90 degrees zenith. It was driven by two amplidyne motors that ran constantly when the turret was turned on and the hand grip (dead man) switch was closed.

The sight was a Sperry computing sight, and it made compensations for trajectory, windage, and the proper lead or trail. When an enemy fighter was in view, the gunner could forget these calculations and align the super-imposed reticule on his target and then adjust the sight for the size of the target. For instance, an ME 109 had a 34-foot wing span, so the gunner would set the dial at 34 feet. Then, with a steady grip, the gunner would turn the handle of the guns to span the fighter plane, track him while keeping him within the framing, and then fire.

The steps are simple, but pulling it off successfully is very difficult. With enough practice in a mock setup, one could get comfortable with the process on the ground, but the gunner had to experience some time in the air with actual combat to really develop the skill. So, if the Good Lord saw fit for you to live through a few fights, you would have a chance to master it.

The pilot is your best friend or your worst enemy when you are not flying in formation. Bill Clark was a master of the art at holding the ship as steady as possible when he knew that I was about to shoot.

Of course, it was important to every gunner on the ship, but it had a greater effect on my aim since the top turret guns had the longest range. In formation with the ship rolling and pitching and constantly changing speeds, it was next to impossible to hit anything. I'd try, but in my estimation few bullets hit the incoming plane unless it came within 400 or 500 yards of us.

Now back to describing the turret. It was compact almost beyond belief when you were bundled up the way we were. With long underwear, heated coveralls, and then a coat, a man could hardly move. Although I was six-foot tall, I was slim and could get into and out of the turret pretty good.

For accommodations there was a metal plate about fourteen inches across that you stood on. And you would stand on that aluminum plate anywhere from four hours up to eight or ten. You couldn't wear a helmet or a flak jacket. And no top or ball turret gunners could wear a parachute.

Otherwise, the turret was completely self-contained. It held nine hundred cartridges for the two big guns – four hundred and fifty on each side. There was a plug-in for your oxygen, an electrical outlet for your heated suit, and of course the microphone cord. None of this hindered the rotation or movement of the turret in any direction.

A very important feature of the turret was the 8mm camera that photographed what was in view anytime your guns were running. The camera was loaded with film that was already labeled with the gunner's position and name and included the airplane's number. These films would be reviewed by the photo lab personnel. The films were shown in the interrogation room on specified days.

Anyone that was available and wanted to was allowed to sit in on the viewing.

Also, there were a few safety features. If your guns were pointed at the tail or wing tip, a fire cut-off switch was automatically engaged to prevent the gunner from firing. If you fired a long burst of shells, the guns would get so hot that a round could "cook-off" and fire even after you stopped shooting. So even with the automatic cut-off switch the gunner had to be very cautious while pivoting toward the wing tips, propellers, or the tail. In addition, a seat belt was provided, but I very quickly decided to remove mine. It was too easy for the belt to trap a man in the event of an emergency.

The top turret wasn't uncomfortable and it was easy to see out of. You usually had a designated area to cover, so working the guns wasn't too tiring. But after several hours of standing in one place with no room to shift your legs or change positions, you would get cramped. Gunners would leave their turrets when they had the chance. My job as flight engineer allowed me occasional opportunities to take breaks to conduct periodic checks on airplane systems or sometimes perform an actual repair. These instances still didn't offer enough relief, though, and usually created stress of a different kind.

He prepares me for battle; he strengthens me to draw a bow
of bronze. You have given me the shield of your salvation.
Your right hand supports me;...
You have made a wide path for my feet to keep them from
slipping. I chased my enemies and caught them;
I did not stop until they were conquered.
Psalm 18:34-37 NLT

Photo Gallery

I would occasionally fly with another crew as the replacement flight engineer. Following are photos are of these planes – some include the original crew members:

USAAF Photo - Declassified
Oral F. Lindsey's Personal Photo Collection

USAAF Photo - Declassified
Oral F. Lindsey's Personal Photo Collection

Other Planes from the 385th Bomb Group

USAAF Photo - Declassified
Oral F. Lindsey's Personal Photo Collection

USAAF Photo - Declassified
Oral F. Lindsey's Personal Photo Collection

USAAF Photo - Declassified
Oral F. Lindsey's Personal Photo Collection

A Soldier's Poems

Introduction

The selection of poems following were previously published in a limited edition although never marketed. The value of this literary work began to be realized once the poetry was exposed to Col. Robert Wood of the Commemorative Air Force by Mr. Lindsey's daughter, Ruby Taylor. With the encouragement of other members of CAF and history buffs alike a second publication of the poetry was pursued. Once that step was taken it became clear that a compilation of literary material would be of greater value to a much larger sector of the populace. And, so, the Top Turret was born.

Oral Lindsey wrote *The Straggler* in 1944 and all other poems in 1946.

Virginia L. Norton

He will remove all of their sorrows, and there will be
no more death or sorrow or crying or pain.
For the old world and its evils are gone forever.
Revelations 21:4 NLT

Straggler

I saw a fort shot out of its group,
Afire and in despair,
With German fighters surrounding it
As it flew alone back there.

The Messerschmitts came barreling through,
Throwing a hail of lead
At a crippled fort that wouldn't quit,
Though it had two engines dead.

Four times a fighter trailed fire and smoke,
Four times a fighter went down.
The fire in the fort had now gone out
And the nerve of the crew was sound.

But time after time the fighters came
To attack the lagging plane.
So I knew her time in the air was short
And my heart was touched to pain.

But the fort stayed up under heavy attack
'Till half her guns were still,
And a fighter seeing the guns were out
Came close to make the kill.

Then a direct hit with the cannon shells

Caused the fort to break in two,

And somewhere the Angels prepared a place

For a weary fortress crew.

*And we know that God causes everything
to work together for the good of those who love God
and are called according to his purpose for them.
Romans 8:28 NLT*

Combat Crew

I want to write the story
Of our old combat crew,
And Al and Roy, my two best friends,
I'm writing it for you.

We trained here in the good old U.S.A.
And our friendship grew very dear,
For even in training we needed help
And death was often near.

We lost one good and Christian pal
In a crack-up at Spokane,
And we'll meet him up in Heaven
When we have crossed the span.

Arthur was better than the rest of us
And I'm sure he was ready to die,
So the Angels called him early
For service in another sky.

Our co-pilot, Lieutenant Jennings,
Was badly hurt that day,
And Bill got a two foot gash down his back
When a tree was in his way.

More training and preparations
Then we crossed the ocean wide
And joined the "Fighting 385th"
On the other side.

From hundreds of write-ups and rumors,
We knew it was a plenty rough show,
But that's where our crew and B-17
Were built and trained to go.

To speak my honest opinion, Al,
Our crew was the very best;
We came from all over the U.S.A.,
From the East coast to the West.

From Kentucky, Bill Clark, our pilot, came
Never a man as good was made,
And he proved how truly good he was
On his last and toughest raid.

Co-Pilot Starr, from California,
Had been wealthy all his life;
He had everything one could wish for,
Including a beautiful wife.

Yes, Paul had given up an awful lot
To go away and fight,
But he had it all to fight for,
So I guess it was only right.

Schleusener, our navigator,
Could guide a fort home like a dream,
But in the blackout over Piccadilly
He had let us drift off the beam.

His home was in Pender, Nebraska,
Near the center of the United States;
If you notice how well we were scattered,
You'll wonder how we got to be mates.

From Missouri came Dick Wheaton, our bombardier,
Who was a real good "Joe,"
And plenty good at finding his target
As all of you fellows know.

Harry Sanders from Pittsburgh
Was at home in the Radio Room,
Sending code or throwing out confetti
Or just listening to the shells go boom!

Leach was our ball gunner,

A good sport in fight or fun,

But he'd rather be in Massachusetts

Where he did not need a gun.

Al Baumann and Roy Bevins

Will always remember how cold

That it could get in the waist of a B-17,

Though in words it cannot be told.

Roy from Virginia and Al from Ohio

Were as close as pals can be,

And the best two pals I've ever had;

They mean the world to me.

The 45th Infantry Division

Lost a strong and hearty man

When Johnny came to the Air Corps

And joined our little band.

Johnny's home was in Oklahoma

And he had lived in Texas too;

He was wide awake as a tail gunner

And a great help to the crew.

They called me Tex, and it was my job
To be their flight engineer;
But with a crew like that and a pair of guns,
I did not have much to fear.

No, I didn't feel that way about it,
For I knew it was only God's will
That stood between me and a bullet
When a fighter came in for the kill.

We often thought of the folks at home
And knew their prayers were sincere,
And I think God forgave our mischief for them
And protected us from fear.

But the flak shells could not distinguish
A good crew of men from the bad,
And the number of killed, wounded, or missing
Would make the strongest feel sad.

And, of course, there were other troubles
That could be as bad as the flak,
For an engine could set fire to a gas tank
And you could bet that one didn't come back.

The cold was as vicious as "Jerry,"
For it was sixty degrees below.
What a rough time for your heat to go off,
But it did sometimes, you know.

With six or eight machine guns
All firing straight ahead,
The fighter has the advantage
When it comes to exchanging lead.

He flies straight toward his target
Or gives it a "duck-shot" lead;
The angle from which he makes the attack
Determines where he'll draw a bead.

At four or five-hundred miles an hour,
He attacks at his very will
Or waits out of gun range and chooses
His best chance to come in for the kill.

When he comes in with all guns blazing
And the bullets tear through your plane,
Death often seems so near to you
That all hopes seem to be in vain.

But the best worldly consolation
Is when you realize he is only a man.
If he can face the machine guns,
You know that you also can.

Everything we hauled was explosive,
From oxygen to gas and bombs,
So it did not give us any comfort
When the flak beat a tune like tom-toms.

Bremen was our first mission
With flak so heavy it was like a screen,
And looking back through memory,
I can say it is still the worst I've seen.

We were sent to the docks at Bremen again
And Ludwigshafen's gas works too,
Along with a target down at Belmesnel;
All were visited by our crew.

Next the cross-bow target,
The Buzz-Bomb launching racks,
And then on to Wilhelmshaven
Where we bombed the railroad tracks.

Dick led the raid on St. Andre, France,
And hit the hangars there;
These last ones, I thought, were not so rough
And the deal seemed almost fair.

Two days later at Frankfurt,
We bombed the Focke Wulf den;
Just two more days and at Brunswick,
We were fighting hard to win.

The Air Force claimed a heavy toll
Of Nazis planes that day,
And the target really took a beating,
Intelligence officers say.

But the Air Force paid a purchase price
In planes and lives of men,
For that is the cost of fighting,
And we were lucky yet to win.

Rostock shook like jelly
As our thousand-pounders fell.
Next we went to Tutow
And gave the Germans hell.

It was the third of March in Forty-four
When we started to Berlin,
But clouds were so high we turned back
And on the fourth we tried again.

On March the eighth the weather faired
And we finally made the grade;
Bombers and Fighters were in battle-dress,
Ready for a long and mighty raid.

The Mustangs really showed their teeth
And the Focke Wulf lost the day;
I did not even fire my guns,
For they kept the Krauts away.

Also, the Lightnings and Thunderbolts
Rode hard on us that trip,
And through the flak and fighters,
Our group never lost a ship.

Dick Wheaton led again that day
And you bet his bombs fell true;
The electric works burned to the ground
And it was a big one too.

Yes, the Mustangs really won the day;
I've never seen such a fight.
The Messerschmitt and Focke Wulf
Were falling left and right.

A successful raid on Berlin
Left us feeling pretty sure;
The next town beneath our open bomb bays
Was Munster in the Valley Ruhr.

Brunswick was hit again in March
Without too much fighters and flak;
Next day we went to Augsburg
And had bandits there and back.

Munich, down near Switzerland,
Proved not too far to go,
And the Alps looked very beautiful
All covered with ice and snow.

Both of these last two missions
Had more color than a wild-west show;
The fire and smoke of battle
On a beautiful scene below.

The puffs of flak and rockets
And red-tailed tracers too.
A German plane broke into flames
Against a sky of azure blue.

Ten snow white chutes were streaming
From a badly crippled fort,
While the Kraut that just had made the kill
Held his fire like a real good sport.

A tail gunner out at three o'clock
Tore a wing off an '88
While a 109 came rolling in
And shot at our plane and another mate.

Again we went to Frankfurt,
Still sore from recent blows;
Chartres was the last we hit in March,
But that was enough I suppose.

Except for occasional air raid alarms,
The next few days were quiet;
Planes were repaired and replacements made
And our duties were few and light.

Then April the ninth it started again
And Warnemunde was first,
And for flying missions long and fast,
The next four raids were the worst.

Next day we went to Diest-Schaffen
And the next, way up to Politz;
Eleven and a half hours in the air,
Boy, how they were running this blitz!

One day of rest then Augsburg
Was slated for an attack,
And out of our squadron alone,
Three planes failed to come back.

On other raids we had lost five,
So this wouldn't have been too bad;
But the loss of our pals on Jorgison's crew
Was what made us feel so sad.

But they'd made it okay to Switzerland
With an engine torn out of the nacelle.
The other two planes that didn't return
Did not get by so well.

Our own fortress took a beating that day
From the One-Fifty-Five's,
And looking at holes in the gas tanks,
We were lucky to escape with our lives.

The long and weary hours
Up there in bitter cold
With an occasional flash of excitement,
Then suspense as yet untold.

From the strain of many missions
Our crew was needing a rest,
And to prove our country worthy,
We got the very best.

We spent ten days in the Palace Hotel
At Southport by the sea
And were as far from combat there
As anyone could be.

It was a real rest and relaxation
And made us want more to live,
But now our rest was over
And again our turn to give.

Just three more trips to Nazi land
And I alone was through
And safely back on English soil,
But not the rest of the crew.

Then the twenty-ninth of April
(It was to be Bill's last trip)
Berlin was to be the target,
Old 109 was the ship.

A jinx ship I had called it,
For it had a bad record for hits
And the engines had enough gremlins
To give a whole ground crew fits.

But the ground crew had worked hard on it
And swore it was now a new crate,
That now they'd tuned up the engines
It ought to perform first rate.

The boys took off that morning
For the worst target Germany had.
I waited long for word from them
But then the news was bad.

"They never reached the target,"
The dry-eyed gunner said,
And almost in a panic
I asked, "Do you think they're all dead?"

"I couldn't tell you yes or no,
But they put up a beautiful scrap;
About thirty enemy fighters
Piled right into their lap.

"They had one engine feathered,
But their guns all seemed okay;
They probably bailed out over Germany.
I doubt that any got away."

The forts were bristling with armament
And their number told their might;
With a great escort expected,
They were spoiling for a fight.

But the fighters were intercepted
And the bombers flew on alone;
The cold seemed even more bitter,
And the engines seemed to moan.

Al was flying as toggelier
And saw the fighters come in.
At first it seemed like a flock of birds,
But the battle soon began.

His guns began to stutter
And the fort began to shake;
Then he heard a crackling shatter
As a Messerschmitt gave them a rake.

Old "One O Nine" took a column of steel
That killed an engine outright,
And with another trying hard to quit,
They were soon alone in the fight.

Bill's voice was on the intercom,
"Get the bombs all out of the bay!"
Al left his guns a moment;
And the bombs were all away.

One prop was feathered out by now
And the crew was on its toes,
As the fighters hit them hard and fast
From tail and wing and nose.

The flame from Johnny's tail guns
Converged in terrific heat;
His eyes grew cold and narrow,
For he was in a deadly seat.

He knocked one fighter down that day
And dodged a lot of lead,
But things was turning for the worse
With another engine dead.

With two engines dead on one side
And 400 miles from home,
With a score of fighters attacking them,
They tried to come back alone.

Then Leach and Schleusener each got a plane
And Leroy took one down too,
And Harry had one trailing smoke –
That went down he almost knew.

Before Al's blazing turret,
Another went down in flame
And the Nazis felt a wave of fear
Against their desire for fame.

All of the boys were shaken by now,
But not a cowardly word nor deed,
And Bill and Starr were fighting hard
To hold their flying speed.

Again, Bill's voice was in every ear
And the crew was tense and still.
They were ready now to fight or flee;
His words would bend their will.

"Boys, we've got two engines left
And I'm going to fly her home.
So how many want to fight it out?
I don't want to go it alone."

Each man in turn paid his tribute
To a worthy skipper's plea
And from every gun position came,
"You bet you can count on me."

At base I watched the planes come in
And the count was still eight low.
When a crippled fort came full in view,
My eyes grew wide, I know.

I knew it was them as they came in low
By the numbers on the tail;
She had two engines dead on one side
And it wasn't too late to fail.

But good ole Bill, he set her down
As easy as a rocking chair.
I couldn't believe they were all okay;
I guess I did not dare.

But those guys couldn't be heroes
Even if they had wanted to;
Not one was wounded, not even a scratch
Though hundreds of slugs went through!

God knows when we are overwhelmed,
And nothing is impossible with Him.
If you don't believe they called for help,
You just ask one of them.

For I am persuaded, that neither death, nor life, nor angels, nor
principalities, nor powers, nor things present, nor things to come;
Nor height, nor depth, nor any other creature, shall be able to
seperate us from the love of God which is in Christ Jesus our Lord.
Romans 8:38, 39 KJV

A Little Boy's Dream

When I was just a little boy
The older lads would tell
Of what they someday hoped to be;
I still remember well.

Then one day a sailor
Chanced to come my way,
And as I listened to his stories,
My heart was light and gay.

For he told of raging sea storms,
Of battles fought at sea,
And he said, "Me lad, the greatest thing's,
A sailor is really free!"

He said, "My home was Norway,
But so many years at sea,
I barely speak my native tongue
But a happy man I be."

He told of the wonders of the deep,
Of fish that really fly,
And the far Pacific Islands
Beneath a starry sky.

"Why, I've been from Cape Horn way down south,
To Alaska's northernmost tip,
And all the way around the world
In many and many a ship.

In whalers and freighters and tankers,
On passenger and warships too,
Beneath at least a dozen flags
And many a different crew.

The girls we met were the fairest yet,
All Sirens of the sea!
And the fairest one in Oslo dwelled,
And her love was just for me.

Aye! Give me a vessel, a rolling deck,
And a million miles o' blue.
The sea has called to many a man,
And lad, she calls for you!"

Well the years went by so swiftly,
And I put out to sea,
And went the ways my friend had gone,
And lived the life so free.

But life grew dull and I grew sad
As we crossed the old North Sea,
When I thought of the old Norwegian,
His name came back to me.

Well I found him up in Oslo,
And he said he had left the sea
To marry the beautiful lady
That he had described to me.

Now, I recall a lady
On a not-too-distant shore,
And a promise I had made her
That I would sail no more.

I'll find my lady by the sea
Then build my life anew,
But I'll always miss the open sea,
And the ship and hearty crew.

The man who finds a wife finds a treasure
and receives favor from the Lord.
Proverbs 18:22 NLT

For God so loved the world that he gave his only Son,
so that everyone who believes in him will not perish but have
eternal life.
John 3:16 NLT

A True Friend

You always love a friend that's true,
The one that cares the most for you.

A friend is one who'll take your place
When danger stares you in the face.

When others try to ruin your name,
A friend sees only greater fame.

Now first, you have to know the man,
Then work out friendship as you can.

But suppose this man has first known you
And dislikes your ways and what you do

But still loves you with all his might
And wants to see you do the right.

Christ is our best, our greatest friend;
Listen and all your doubts will end.

He lived and died without doing a wrong.
With patience and mercy he suffered long.

He healed the sick, consoled the distressed,
And those that believed Him were greatly blessed.

He loved our souls and hated none,
His every deed proved him God's own Son.

Yes, He healed the sick, a wonderful deed,
But he came to provide for our greatest need.

This life is short, our souls live on;
A few years on Earth and our chance is gone.

Christ alone can save us from hell;
We all have sinned, you know too well.

But He gave His life that we might live –
The greatest gift He had to give.

Now believe in Him and the plan is complete;
We must humble ourselves at the Master's feet.

You need no excuse and His grace is free;
His love for your soul is as deep as the sea.

So trust my Friend, the Lamb of Love,
And spend eternity in Heaven above.

From the Author

Author's Testimony

There was a lot of talk those days about fear and bravery in war. Fear can be a terrible thing. On the one extreme it can be paralyzing, preventing you from any action. But it is an instinct built into all of us to guard us from danger and to temper our decisions. Some people said I had no fear or that I was just crazy. If that's true, then there were a lot of crazy men.

I attribute my so-called lack of fear to a specific event in my life that changed my heart and my outlook. I was twelve years old when our little country church, Bethel Baptist, had a revival. At the time, I believed that I was already a Christian, so I assumed the preacher was talking to those "other" people who didn't love God.

During the revival I heard Brother Campbell as he preached and quoted the scripture, "All have sinned and come short of the Glory of God." Even though I considered myself a Christian, I knew that I wasn't perfect, so I began to listen intently. The preacher went on to explain that because of this sin, all of us needed forgiveness to be able to enter the gates of Heaven.

The truth came ringing through loud and clear. Suddenly, I was the worst sinner that ever lived. I knew that I had never asked for that forgiveness that is given freely by the Lord for those that put their trust in Him. As His word says, "It is by grace through faith that a man is saved and not by works lest any man should boast."

Brother Campbell said that there was no sin that God could not forgive, and He would if you came to Him seriously seeking forgiveness. I was very serious and did want what God had to offer. When I realized my sin and asked God to forgive me and make Jesus the Lord of my life, He gave me a lot more than forgiveness and the promise of Heaven. You see, I had been such a wimp as a child. I feared everyone and everything. But that night I was changed, spiritually and mentally, and I realized that I wasn't afraid anymore.

God always blesses each of us with special skills and gifts. What was given to me was the ability to face the world without fear. Oh, I still had the survival kind of fear, but I approached life with an attitude of confidence instead of fear. Because of this life-changing experience I was able to think clearly in the face of gunfire – even when fighting was heaviest and flak was bursting all around.

Some people confuse patient observation with being slow-witted. So one of the first things I told my pilot, Captain Clark, was, "Sometimes it may look like I'm confused, because I'll take longer to make a decision than some folks. So give me a minute to look things over, read the instruments, and then I'll calculate the odds."

He was a West Point graduate and he said, "That's not being slow, that's using common sense."

The reality is no one can be prepared for everything that can possibly happen. That's why I simply used everything God had blessed me with and then looked to Him to handle the rest. I prayed for guidance and protection, not just for me, but the whole crew. I prayed for the nightmare to end.

It wasn't just my prayers that spared my life and others. It was the prayers of my family, of countless other families, and of congregations in churches all over the world who poured out their petitions to our Father in Heaven.

The Lord is my light and my salvation
— so why should I be afraid?
The Lord protects me from danger — so why should I tremble?
Though a mighty army surrounds me, my heart will know no fear.
Even if they attack me, I remain confident.
Psalm 27:1,3 NLT

When We Were Young

Oral Franklin Lindsey 1946 - Age 24

In Loving Memory

Roberta Alice Lindsey

My Loving Wife of 57 Years

1930 - 2003

In Loving Memory

Parents – John F. and Elmina Lindsey
Stamford, Texas March 1949

HEADQUARTERS
43RD BOMBARDMENT WING (MEDIUM)
UNITED STATES AIR FORCE
CARSWELL AIR FORCE BASE, TEXAS

REPLY TO
ATTN OF: 43C

31 October 1963

SUBJECT: Letter of Appreciation

TO: TSgt Oral F. Lindsey, AF38230452
43 Organizational Maintenance Squadron
43 Bomb Wing (SAC)
Carswell AFB, Texas

Dear Sergeant Lindsey

1. It is with great pleasure and sincerity that I write
this letter to you in recognition of your more than twenty
years of honorable and faithful service to our country.
Through your sacrifices and the sacrifices of thousands of
men like you, our country has emerged victorious in every
conflict in which we became engaged.

2. It is my intent that by receipt of this letter you
may know that your service has truly been appreciated
by your fellow citizens. It is my hope that your service
years have been as worth while and meaningful to you as
they have been to those for whom you served.

3. Although you will no longer be on active duty serving
your country, I want you to know that we will continue to
regard you as a member of our Air Force family.

Sincerely

E. W. HOLSTROM
Colonel, USAF
Commander

PEACE IS OUR PROFESSION

About The Author

Oral F. Lindsey was the seventh of seven children born to a farming family in Anson, Texas. He became interested in being an engineer after reading a news article about Boeing's development of the B-10 Bomber. Without the proper education to fill this position he decided to enlist during WWII and serve wherever he would be qualified. The determination of his quest with God's blessings took him through amazing adventures in training and through two combat tours in the European Theatre of Operations. Through the providence of God he was blessed with his dream and survived to share those adventures with the world.

Printed in the United States
27647LVS00002B/49-558